506·85

AS/A-LEVEL YEAR 1

STUDENT GUIDE

AQA

Sociology

Families and households

Joan Garrod

1 8   2015

D0783982

Philip Allan, an imprint of Hodder Education, an Hachette UK company, Blenheim Court, George Street, Banbury, Oxfordshire OX16 5BH

Orders

Bookpoint Ltd, 130 Milton Park, Abingdon, Oxfordshire OX14 4SB

tel: 01235 827827

fax: 01235 400401

e-mail: education@bookpoint.co.uk

Lines are open 9.00 a.m.–5.00 p.m., Monday to Saturday, with a 24-hour message answering service. You can also order through the Hodder Education website: www.hoddereducation.co.uk

© Joan Garrod 2015

ISBN 978-1-4718-4435-5

First printed 2015

Impression number 5 4 3 2 1

Year 2019 2018 2017 2016 2015

This Guide has been written specifically to support students preparing for the AQA AS and A-level Sociology examinations. The content has been neither approved nor endorsed by AQA and remains the sole responsibility of the author.

Typeset by Integra Software Services Pvt. Ltd., Pondicherry, India

Cover photo: Marco Govel/Fotolia

Printed in Italy

Hachette UK's policy is to use papers that are natural, renewable and recyclable products and made from wood grown in sustainable forests. The logging and manufacturing processes are expected to conform to the environmental regulations of the country of origin.

Contents

Content Guidance

Questions & Answers

■ Getting the most from this book

Exam tips

Advice on key points in the text to help you learn and recall content, avoid pitfalls, and polish your exam technique in order to boost your grade.

Knowledge check

Rapid-fire questions throughout the Content Guidance section to check your understanding.

Knowledge check answers

1 Turn to the back of the book for the Knowledge check answers.

Summaries

■ Each core topic is rounded off by a bullet-list summary for quick-check reference of what you need to know.

Exam-style questions →

Commentary on the questions

Tips on what you need to do to gain full marks, indicated by the icon **e**

Sample student answers

Practise the questions, then look at the student answers that follow.

Question 2

1 Define the term 'fertility rate'. [2 marks]

e There are several 'rates' in discussion of populations – make sure you choose the right one.

2 Using one example, briefly explain how the modern family could be seen as patriarchal. [2 marks]

e Note that the question is talking about the modern family, not families in the nineteenth century.

3 Outline three reasons for the increase in cohabitation. [6 marks]

e Remember that you are asked to 'outline' the reasons – write enough to gain the marks, but avoid lengthy discussions. Put each reason on a new line.

4 Outline and explain two ways in which our ideas of 'childhood' have changed. [10 marks]

e This is almost a 'compare and contrast' type of question, so for each way you should say how it was in the past and how it has changed. As there are 10 marks available, you could say something brief about why the changes have occurred.

5 Read Item B below and answer the question that follows.

Item B

Many functions that were once carried out by the family, such as the welfare of its members, have been taken over by agencies such as the medical profession and social services. However, the family still performs some essential functions, such as socialising children and producing the next generation.

Applying material from Item B and your knowledge, evaluate the view that the state has taken over most of the functions of the family. [20 marks]

e Remember to identify the material from the Item that you must use – you have been given an example of a family function now taken over by other bodies and examples of functions that are still carried out by the family. Your knowledge should enable you to add to these. Evaluation should be shown by assessing, with examples and evidence, whether and to what extent the view expressed in the question can be upheld. Always remember the danger of talking about 'the family' as though all families were the same.

Student A

1 The fertility rate is the number of live births per 1,000 women of child-bearing age (15–45) per year in a population.

e 2/2 marks awarded. This is concise and correct.

Commentary on sample student answers

Find out how many marks each answer would be awarded in the exam and then read the comments (preceded by the icon **e**) following each student answer. Annotations that link back to points made in the student answers show exactly how and where marks are gained or lost.

■About this book

This guide covers the topic of *Families and households* in the AQA specifications 7191 (AS) and 7192 (A-level). The content is identical for both, but A-level students will be expected to demonstrate a greater knowledge and understanding of sociological theory. The structure of the examination is also different for AS and A-level, so when you come to read through the questions, it is important that you note which are the correct ones for your course, though you may, of course, wish to use the others for revision or exam practice. Remember that this is a guide, not a textbook. It indicates and briefly explains and discusses those things that you should know and understand about this topic but is intended to complement, not replace, your textbooks and class notes.

How to use the book

The first main section of the book is **Content Guidance**. It follows the headings for this topic and the sequence in which they occur in the AQA specification, but it is not necessary to read them in this order, provided that you make sure that you cover them all.

In your study of this topic area you should examine the two **core themes**. These are:
- socialisation, culture and identity
- social differentiation, power and stratification.

These are not things to be studied separately – rather, in your study of *Families and households* you should be aware of the two core themes running through the topic.

You should also be aware of both the **evidence** of, and the **sociological explanations** for, the content of this topic. This means that you must study the relevant sociological theories, perspectives and methods associated with this topic, as well as the design of the research used to obtain any data under consideration, including their strengths and limitations.

The specification also states that 'students should be encouraged to use examples drawn from their own experience of small-scale research'. Note that this is not a requirement but a recommendation. Your teacher may provide you with some research exercises, but the Content Guidance section also makes a few suggestions of tasks that you could undertake that would give you experience of different research methods around the topic of *Families and households*. These can be found in tinted boxes at the end of a section.

Each section of the Content Guidance contains exam tips, knowledge checks and definitions of some key terms. Knowing and understanding the meaning of sociological concepts is an essential part of the whole course.

The second main section of the book is that of **Questions & Answers**. At the beginning of this section are the three assessment objectives against which your exam answers will be judged, with some guidance regarding how to display the required skills, and also a list of command words, which will help you to understand more clearly what each question is asking you to do. The questions provided are in the style of the AQA exam for this topic, and are divided into AS and A-level questions, each with two student answers, one from a student whose answer is at the level of an A grade, and one from a student whose answer is at roughly a C grade. Remember the importance of noting the structure and mark allocations of questions at the appropriate level for you, either AS or A-level. However, given that the content is the same, there is no harm in writing answers to all the questions given here – just remember when you look at the marks awarded and read the comments that they are being applied to a particular level, either AS or A-level. Throughout the student answers, you will find comments, explaining why what has been written is good and is scoring well, and where things have gone wrong or there is room for improvement. More detailed guidance on how to use the Questions & Answers section is given at the beginning of that section.

Content Guidance

■ The relationship of the family to the social structure and social changes

All sociologists agree that the family is a very important part of the **social structure**, but there are disagreements about the role that the family plays for individuals and for society. It is useful to group together sociologists with like ideas, but also important to remember that there can be disagreements within, as well as between, these groups.

It is acknowledged that one of the main purposes, or functions, of the family is that of **primary socialisation**. However, there are disagreements about the wider role played by the family, and also how and why it has changed over time.

Functionalist view of the family

To a functionalist, all the institutions of society contribute to the stability and well-being of that society. It is acknowledged that sometimes things change or go wrong, and an institution or part of it becomes dysfunctional, but the normal state is that all institutions function in a positive way. Functionalism is a structural theory, meaning that its analysis is based on the level of society as a whole, rather than the individual. It looks at the interrelationship of the different parts of society, to see how they fit together to benefit society as a whole. Some functional views of the role of the family in society are based on **anthropology**.

> **Anthropology** The study of humans, past and present. Much anthropological research is based on small-scale non-industrial societies or small groups within a society. A debate within sociology is the extent to which the findings of such studies can be applied to large industrial societies.

George Murdoch

Anthropologist George Murdoch, writing in 1949, published research from his study of a sample of 250 societies, from groups of hunter-gatherers, through small-scale agricultural societies to large-scale industrial societies, including America. He concluded that even though there were different family forms, at the heart of every

Social structure
The social institutions in a society (e.g. the education system, religious organisations) and also the patterns of social relationships between people and groups (e.g. the class structure, kinship networks).

Primary socialisation
This occurs mainly in early childhood and is the learning of the language, norms, values and roles of a society.

Knowledge check 1
If primary socialisation takes place largely within the family, where does secondary socialisation take place?

family – the nucleus – were a man and a woman and their child or children. This common nucleus was what he termed 'the nuclear family', which was based on:

- common residence
- economic cooperation
- reproduction

Murdoch thus concluded that the nuclear family was 'a universal social grouping'.

Murdoch believed that the nuclear family performed four basic functions for society. These were:

- sexual – it was a way of regulating people's sexual behaviour in a socially acceptable manner
- reproductive – it ensured that children were born to a couple who had responsibility to care for them, hence ensuring the continuation of society
- economic – the family was a unit which met the basic needs of its members for food, clothing and shelter. In many societies, the family produced goods for its members and for the wider society – it was a unit of production
- educational – within the family, children would be taught the norms and values of their society, together with any necessary essential skills. Murdoch was actually referring to primary socialisation

Talcott Parsons

Parsons was an American sociologist. Writing in the 1950s, he considered that the nuclear family had become more specialised and had shed some of its earlier functions, which were now taken over or shared by other bodies in society, such as the education system. Parsons thought that modern nuclear families performed two essential functions for society. These were:

- the primary socialisation of children
- the stabilisation of the adult personality – this meant that families provided a safe haven for adults, helping them to cope with the stresses and strains of modern living

Parsons is particularly well known for his views on role allocation within the family. He believed that the family operated most efficiently, was most stable and was most beneficial to society when there was a clear-cut **division of labour** between the two adult partners – who were, of course, seen as a male and a female. Parsons said that the male and female should play what he saw as their 'natural' roles, which complemented each other. The male role was the instrumental role, by which he meant to be the breadwinner. The female role was the expressive role, caring for and nurturing the children and looking after the home. Parsons believed that the sharing of family roles in this way ensured family stability.

Knowledge check 3

To what extent do you think that the idea that the instrumental and expressive roles for males and females are 'natural' is supported by the evidence?

Knowledge check 2

What family forms can you identify that do not correspond to Murdoch's definition of the universal nuclear family?

Division of labour The way in which work is allocated. In the context of the family, it refers to how paid work, domestic work and childcare are divided up between family members – who typically does what, or is expected to do what.

Evaluation

+ Draws attention to the importance of the family as an institution in society.
+ Shows how the family links to the economy.
+ Shows the positive side of family life for individuals and for society.
- Fails to recognise alternative family forms.
- Model based on traditional white middle-class family.
- Does not fully consider that other institutions might fulfil some functions, e.g. socialisation.
- Sees the division of labour between the sexes as 'natural' rather than learned behaviour.
- Ignores negative effects such as domestic violence, subordination of women.

New Right views of the family

New Right views are primarily political, rather than sociological, and have had a significant influence on British social policies on the family introduced under Conservative and coalition governments. Where the family is concerned, one name in particular is associated with New Right views.

Charles Murray

Like other New Right thinkers, Murray is concerned with what he sees as the negative effects caused to individuals and to society by the breakdown of the so-called traditional nuclear family. This breakdown is evidenced by issues such as the rising rates of cohabitation, divorce and single parenthood, and the growth of a **culture of dependency** which is passed down through the generations. Murray believes that too-generous welfare benefits are largely to blame for many of society's ills.

The New Right emphasises the virtue of individualism, of people looking after themselves and their family with the minimum of state intervention. Former prime minister Margaret Thatcher referred to such intervention as 'the nanny state'. Murray is known for his development of the concept of 'the underclass', though this is often misinterpreted as referring to those in poverty. In an article in 2000 for *The Sunday Times*, 'Underclass + 10', Murray clarified this. He wrote: 'By underclass, I do not mean people who are merely poor, but people at the margins of society, unsocialised and often violent.' Murray's view was that families in the underclass were characterised by what he saw as deviant attitudes towards parenting, work and crime.

Culture of dependency
An alleged set of values brought about by over-generous welfare benefits, leading recipients to rely on 'handouts' from the state rather than finding work and providing for themselves and their children.

Evaluation

+ Draws attention to some of the negative effects of family breakdown for individuals and society.
− Political, rather than sociological, view.
− Sees all changes to the traditional nuclear family as negative.
− Blames working-class problems on too-generous welfare benefits.
− Fails to recognise other factors that can cause family problems and breakdown, such as domestic violence, unemployment, low wages, poor housing, racism.
− No evidence for existence of 'underclass'.

Marxist views of the family

As well as 'classical' Marxist views on the family, many sociologists, such as some feminists, take a Marxist approach.

Friedrich Engels

Early Marxist writings on the family come not from Marx but from Engels, whose ideas were expressed in his book *The Origin of the Family, Private Property and the State*, published in 1884. In summary, Engels believed that family structure evolved over time, and the monogamous nuclear family developed with the emergence of a class society based on private property. He said that before this, property was held by the community, rather than by individuals, and adults were free to choose sexual partners at will.

With the development of **capitalism**, some people began to acquire property and wealth, which they wished to pass down to their heirs, particularly their sons. To do this, they needed to know who their children were, so the idea of a monogamous nuclear family emerged, with a male head and a female wife who would bear only his children. Engels wrote that the monogamous family was the first in history to be based on economic conditions. With **industrialisation**, the capitalist owners needed their (predominantly male) workers to be looked after and kept healthy for work, and this task fell to the wives within the home, who also provided the emotional support their husbands needed.

Knowledge check 4

What is meant by monogamy?

Eli Zaretsky

Zaretsky, in his book *Capitalism, the Family and Personal Life* (1976), focused on the family as a refuge for individuals, particularly workers, from the alienation caused by capitalism. He said that with industrialisation, the home and the workplace became two distinct spheres, with the family and home being the 'private sphere'. His argument was that as it provided much-needed relief and comfort to people, the nuclear family acted as a major prop to capitalism. In other words, the family performed an 'ideological function'.

Capitalism An economic system in which the ownership of those things that produce wealth (such as businesses, factories, land and property) are largely privately owned.

Industrialisation When a society moves from a predominantly agricultural base to one where the economy is dominated by manufacturing in workshops and factories. Also associated with urbanisation, where many people move to live and work in towns and cities.

The family also served capitalism in other ways:

- through the (unpaid) domestic work of women
- through the reproduction of the labour force
- as an important unit of consumption

Louis Althusser

Althusser saw the family as one of the ideological state apparatuses, that is, those institutions that served capitalism by socialising people into accepting that capitalism and an unequal class society were 'normal'. Values taught within the home, such as obedience, the acceptance of authority, different roles for men and women and so on, were an important part of this socialisation process.

Evaluation

+ Shows a link between family structure and the economy.
+ Takes a critical look at the family.
+ Locates the family within the ideological state apparatus.
- Links everything about the family to the capitalist economic structure – economic determinism.
- Ignores other reasons for marriage, such as romantic love.
- Focuses on the negative aspects of the family.
- Ignores people's subjective experiences of family life.
- By focusing only on capitalism, ignores other forms of oppression, e.g. patriarchy.

Feminist views of the family

There are several feminist views of the family, but most of them take a highly critical look at how the family affects women. A common theme is the focus on the family as an institution involving power relationships.

Marxist feminists

- The main source of the exploitation of women is the capitalist system.
- Women's domestic and childcare work goes unrewarded, yet is essential.
- Wages paid to male workers in effect buy the labour power of two people.
- Women provide the next generation of workers – the social reproduction of labour power.
- Women form a 'reserve army of labour' – called into the labour force when needed, but when not working need no financial reward as they will be supported by their male partner.
- The family teaches children obedience, in preparation for their future role as exploited workers.
- The family socialises children to accept their unequal place in a class-ridden society, and socialises females into accepting their role as subservient to males.

Knowledge check 5

What is meant by the family being a 'unit of consumption'?

Radical feminists

- The main source of the exploitation of women is not capitalism but patriarchy.
- Families are primarily authoritarian units dominated by men.
- Patriarchal ideology suggests that being a wife and mother is the most important female role.
- When women are in paid work, they still have the prime responsibility for domestic and childcare tasks, which imposes a 'double burden'.
- Women also provide the emotional support for family members, which when combined with paid employment and household tasks forms a 'triple shift'.
- Economic and social constraints make it difficult for women to escape the patriarchal family.
- Many disadvantages to women stem from their role as providers of childcare.

Liberal feminists

- It is important to recognise that there has been significant progress for women in recent years.
- There is greater equality in most marriages/partnerships.
- The high rates of remarriage and the formation of new partnerships indicate that women generally have a high commitment to family life.
- Feminists should devise policies to encourage greater equality within relationships, rather than always seeing men as 'the enemy'.
- Employers and governments should introduce policies to help working parents.

Difference feminists

- No one family structure is the same, therefore it is impossible to make claims about the role and functions of families and family members.
- What happens in families is influenced by factors such as social class, ethnicity, generation and sexual orientation.
- The 'family ideology' which sets up the nuclear family as the ideal devalues other types of family structure.
- The emphasis on the caring side of family life neglects the darker side, such as domestic violence and child abuse.
- The nuclear family can be seen as 'anti-social' as members are so focused on the family and family relationships that they neglect wider social contacts.

Evaluation

- \+ Has had a huge impact on how sociologists have studied the family.
- \+ Challenges the traditional view that gendered roles are 'natural'.
- \+ Focuses on patriarchy as inbuilt into society's institutions, including the family.
- \+ Shows the negative side of family life, especially for women.
- − Some views fail to recognise the diversity of family life.
- − Tends to assume that all women are oppressed within the family.
- − Neglects the positive benefits of family life.

Postmodern views of the family

Postmodern views believe that the 'grand narratives' of the modern period, such as Marxism, progress, democracy, etc., are no longer sufficient to explain and make sense of contemporary life. Rather, they see postmodern societies as characterised by fragmentation, diversity, individualism and choice.

There is no longer any single ideal family type. Individuals decide for themselves whether they wish to marry, cohabit or remain alone, whether to have children or not, and what kind of relationship(s) they wish to have. In other words, 'the family' is whatever people choose it to be. Evidence of this is the increasing diversity of family and household structures found in Western societies.

Part of this diversity has arisen because of increasing equality between the sexes. Some research has suggested that women are the main agents of change, as they decide whether or not to marry, have children, continue in paid employment or divorce. It has been suggested that one result of this increase in the assertiveness and social position of women in the family has led to a 'crisis of masculinity', as men struggle to define their role. A darker side of this is the possible increase in domestic violence as some men strive to reassert their dominance and authority over other family members, especially women. Similarly, it is recognised that increasing choice in relationships and marriage patterns can lead to greater instability within families.

Evaluation

+ Draws attention to diversity of family structures.
+ No value judgements on 'best' type of family.
+ Recognises the importance of changes to women's roles.
+ Links changes in families to wider changes such as globalisation and fragmentation of class structure.
− Over-emphasises the degree of choice in people's lives, particularly for some women.
− Does not recognise the importance of tradition and custom and the continuing constraints of class.
− Ignores that most family patterns remain fairly traditional.

The family and the economy

Some sociologists, such as Talcott Parsons, have linked a particular type of family structure to the economy and the prevailing mode of production. The suggestion is that in pre-industrial societies the extended family is the dominant structure, while the twin processes of industrialisation and urbanisation lead to the dominant structure becoming nuclear, as this structure is thought best to meet the needs of the economy.

The suggestion is that when most goods are produced in the home, for example by families working together as outworkers, and in the absence of any kind of state welfare system, large extended families that can work together and look after family members in times of illness, unemployment or old age are the best type. With the move to industrialisation, the economy needs a mobile workforce that can move to where the work is, so smaller units are better. At the same time, the focus moves to a largely male workforce, and the role of women becomes increasingly confined to the domestic sphere. As the state begins to take on some welfare functions, there is less need for the family to provide all the care for its members.

This is sometimes known as the 'fit thesis', as it suggests that one type of family structure best fits a particular economic structure. However, research has shown that the picture is far from as clear-cut as this thesis suggests.

Peter Laslett

Laslett (1972) looked at family and household size and composition in England between 1564 and 1821 and found that only 10% contained kin besides the nuclear family – about the same percentage as in 1966. One of the reasons for this was that the pattern of late marriage and early death made three-generation families more uncommon. Later, Laslett looked at family structure in some other European countries and found the English pattern repeated. This led him to claim that there was a 'Western family' structure that was predominantly nuclear. Rather than the process of industrialisation leading to the spread of nuclear families, Laslett suggested that it was the other way round – the widespread existence of nuclear household structures actually helped the process of industrialisation.

Michael Anderson

Other research that casts doubt on the 'fit thesis' is that carried out by Anderson (1971). If the fit thesis were correct, areas that had undergone industrialisation should have been among the first to have shown the predominance of nuclear families. Anderson carried out research using the 1851 Census for Preston, in Lancashire. He chose Preston as it was a textile town, therefore based on one of the first industries to industrialise, though with sufficient time to have elapsed for any changes in family structure to be apparent.

Using a one-in-ten sample of households, he found that almost a quarter of households (23%) contained kin beyond the nuclear family – in other words, extended families. This co-residence of wider kin was mostly found among the poorer households, and kin were used as an important informal welfare system, supporting each other in a number of ways.

Peter Willmott and Michael Young

Two other writers who saw a link between family structure and composition and the economic structure were Willmott and Young (1974). They saw families as being in four main stages, with the family in stage 3 at their time of writing.

- *Stage 1*: pre-industrial, where the family was a unit of production and extended families were widespread.
- *Stage 2*: early industrial – nuclear families became more common and many families were **matrifocal**.
- *Stage 3*: symmetrical – the welfare state had taken over many of the functions previously performed by families. There was greater geographical mobility, so families often lived at some distance from kin. Fewer children meant that it was

Matrifocal A family in which the mother is seen as the most important member and men play a less important role in the family and childcare.

easier for wives to go out to work, and the effect of two wages allowed more money to be spent on the home and leisure activities. As homes became more comfortable, men grew more 'home centred', with family life becoming increasingly important to them. While household tasks were still gendered to a large extent, the symmetrical family was characterised by men and women spending a more equal amount of time on household-related tasks than previously.

- *Stage 4*: this was in the future. The belief was that as technology reduced the number of routine tasks, people's work (especially that of men) would become more interesting, and their focus and leisure interests would turn outside the home.

Evaluation

+ Important to look at the relationship between the family and other institutions in society, particularly the economy.
- Fails to recognise the importance of class to family and household structure – the aristocracy usually had different patterns of family life and child-bearing from the middle classes, who in turn were different from the poor.
- The 'fit thesis' not borne out by the evidence, which indicates that at any time there is a wide variety of family structures.

The family and social policies

It is important to remember that social policies are governed by **dominant social values**. Therefore social policies on the family will both reflect what is actually happening in society (e.g. a rise in lone parents or teenage pregnancies) and offer a model of what those in power think families *ought* to be like. So some social policies will be aimed at rewarding or promoting what is seen as desirable behaviour, while others will penalise or discourage what is seen as deviant or undesirable behaviour.

There are so many social policies on the family that you will not be expected to know them all in detail. However, you should know the areas of family life that have been the object of state policies and some of the main points – the more recent the better. The following list is a guide:

- *Marriage* – the next section will look at this in more detail, but you should be aware of important changes such as the introduction of civil partnerships and same-sex marriage.
- *Abortion* – laws allowing women (under certain conditions) to terminate a pregnancy.
- *Adoption and fostering* – including issues such as whether children should be placed with families of the same religious/ethnic background as them.
- *Divorce* – under what conditions a divorce can be granted.
- *Lone parents* – benefits to help lone parents.
- *Family breakdown* – arrangements for children following family breakdown, such as maintenance payments, visiting rights, etc.
- *Parenting* – some important policies here, including financial (e.g. child benefit, tax credits) and support (e.g. parenting classes).

Dominant social values Those things such as ideas of right and wrong, what is appropriate behaviour in particular situations, what the role of the state should be, etc. that have a consensus among the majority of people in a society.

- *Education* – free pre-school education, Education Maintenance Allowance, school programmes aimed at promoting desirable social relationships, preventing teenage pregnancies, avoiding domestic violence, etc.
- *Working parents* – maternity/paternity leave, flexible working hours, support with childcare, etc.
- *Health* – ante-natal and maternity care, child immunisation and vaccination programmes, care for the elderly and disabled.

There are different theoretical perspectives on social policies and the family. Remember that within each of these views there are groups with different opinions.

The functionalist view

Functionalists see a stable family as very important for society. Social policies are designed to benefit the whole society. The 'march of progress' theory sees developments in education, health and working practices as helping families to fulfil their important functions of the appropriate socialisation of children and providing a safe and stable environment for adults.

The Marxist view

Marxists view all state social policies as designed to serve the interests of capitalism. Therefore family policies such as supporting parents, making it easier for women to join the labour force (or more difficult if their labour is not needed) are all designed to ensure that capitalism has the workforce that it needs. Policies promoting 'family values' such as obedience and respect for authority are designed to ensure an obedient and compliant future workforce.

The New Right view

New Right thinkers do not approve of too much state intervention in people's lives, including the family. They are against what they see as too-generous benefits to 'deviant' households such as lone parents and non-working households. Their argument is that such benefits will lead to a 'culture of dependency', which will make people over-reliant on the state and rob them of the incentive to find work and engage in lifestyles that are more socially desirable.

Knowledge check 6

In what way could lone parents and non-working households be considered 'deviant'?

The feminist view

Feminists see many social policies as reflecting the 'ideology of familism', that is, promoting a particular view of family structure and life. They are against policies which they see as upholding patriarchy, such as different entitlements for female and male employees following the birth of a child (note that there are now new policies on this), policies that penalise lone parents, most of whom are women, and policies that reflect the view that mothers are primarily responsible for the behaviour of their children. They support policies that benefit women, such as those allowing abortion, making divorce easier, punishing domestic violence and giving legal rights to same-sex partnerships.

Exam tip

Remember that there is no single 'feminist view', although there are some shared beliefs. Showing your knowledge of different types of feminism could gain you additional marks.

Evaluation

+ Without certain social policies, many more families would struggle to 'make ends meet'.
+ School-based programmes could be important in raising issues of domestic violence, teenage pregnancy, good parenting skills, etc.
− Some policies seem to be strongly focused on the traditional nuclear family, to the detriment of other types of family structure.

Key concepts

social structure; primary socialisation; nuclear family; extended family; domestic division of labour; underclass; capitalism; ideological state apparatus; patriarchy; grand narratives; industrialisation; urbanisation; dominant social values

Summary

- All sociologists agree that the family is a very important institution in society.
- There are different theoretical ideas about the exact relationship between the family and the wider social structure.
- Changes in the family both lead to and reflect changes in the wider social structure.
- While family and household structures have been influenced by the processes of industrialisation and urbanisation, there is no proven causal link and it appears that there has always been a variety of family and household structures.
- The family remains an important focus of social policy, though sociologists disagree about the purpose, desirability and effects of different social policies.
- State policies on the family reflect dominant social values.

Knowledge check 7

What is meant by the terms 'industrialisation' and 'urbanisation'?

■ Changing patterns of marriage, cohabitation, separation, divorce, child-bearing and the life course

While the following summarises the main changes, you should be aware that there are differences, often significant ones, between groups based on social class, ethnic group, religion, age and sexual orientation. Note, too, that there are different sociological explanations of these changes and their impact on society. Most of our knowledge of these patterns comes from quantitative data, such as the Census and the registration of births, marriages and deaths. Information about the reasons for the changes, and their impact on the individuals concerned, usually comes from qualitative data such as interviews.

Exam tip

Statements about changes in family roles and structures tend to be general and applied to the whole population. Try to include statements such as 'This trend is seen to a much lesser degree among some minority ethnic communities' or 'The age at which women have their first child tends to be higher among middle-class women'. Make sure that your comments are relevant to the question asked.

Marriage

Britain is a monogamous society, in which people legally can have only one spouse at a time. In all societies, marriage is regulated in some way, with laws or norms governing who may marry whom. Marriage can be either **endogamous** or **exogamous**.

While the choice of a marriage partner in Britain is largely left to the individual, many people marry someone from a broadly similar background to themselves. However, the 2011 Census showed a rise in the number of people married or cohabiting with someone from a different ethnic group. Some British Asians now follow a 'middle route' between the traditional arranged marriages of their cultural background and the totally free choice exercised by most white British people. They do this by using specialist online sites enabling them to find marriage partners according to their own chosen criteria, such as ethnic group, religion, etc.

Although some writers have seen the changes in marriage patterns and the growth in cohabitation and lone parenthood as signalling the 'death of the family', marriage remains a strong institution. The 2011 Census showed that of the 15.8 million families in the UK, 65% were married couples. Despite the increase in marriage followed by divorce and remarriage (**serial monogamy**), in 2013 more than two-thirds of all marriages (67%) were first marriages for both partners, 15% were remarriages for both partners, and 13% were where one of the partners had been previously married.

The average (mean) age of marriage has been rising and is now slightly above 33 years.

The decline in religious practice is evidenced by the fact that 70% of all marriages are now civil, rather than religious, ceremonies.

Under the Civil Partnerships Act of 2004, same-sex couples were able to obtain virtually the same rights as married heterosexual partners. By October 2013 more than 120,000 civil partnerships had been formed.

Under the Marriage (Same Sex Couples) Act of 2013, which came into force in March 2014, same-sex couples in England and Wales could legally marry. Between March and June that year, more than 1,400 such marriages took place. From December 2014, same-sex couples in civil partnerships could convert their partnership to marriage.

Endogamous marriage is where marriage takes place between members of the same tribe, class, religion or ethnic group, either by law or custom.

Exogamous marriage is where people marry someone from outside their group.

Serial monogamy The practice whereby while people have only one spouse at a time, they have a pattern of marriage, divorce and remarriage – sometimes several times.

Exam tip

Remember that despite rises in cohabitation, divorce and lone parenthood, the evidence shows the continuing importance and popularity of marriage as an institution.

Exam tip

Civil partnerships and same-sex marriages are an important change to our traditional ideas of marriage. Make sure that you show your awareness of this.

The Office for National Statistics has identified what it calls **concealed families**. This could refer to a young couple living with one set of parents or an older couple living with an adult child and their family. Almost 2% of all families come into this category, usually for economic or cultural reasons.

While the vast majority of marriages are entered into voluntarily by two adults, the Forced Marriage Unit was created in 2013 to investigate cases where this was not so and found more than 1,300 cases where at least one of the partners was forced into marriage. Forced and child marriages in the UK often take place for religious and cultural reasons and are associated with members of some minority ethnic groups.

> **Concealed families** Families living in a multi-family household.

> **Knowledge check 8**
> What is the difference between a forced marriage and an arranged marriage?

Cohabitation

The 2011 Census showed that 17% of families were cohabiting couples. While for some this may be a permanent state, for many it is a temporary stage. Almost nine out of ten couples who marry have lived together before marriage.

Cohabitation often occurs after a divorce or separation, which explains why more than four out of every ten cohabiting couples are over the age of 40.

One of the reasons for the growth in cohabitation is likely to be the decline in the **stigma** of this arrangement, though the sheer number of couples cohabiting is also an important factor in its growing acceptability.

> **Stigma** Social disapproval.

Separation and divorce

Divorce in England and Wales is now granted on the grounds of 'the irretrievable breakdown of marriage', whereas previously at least one of the partners had to be guilty of something, often adultery.

With every change in the law making divorce easier, the number of divorces has risen, suggesting that some people would have divorced had the law made it possible.

> **Exam tip**
> You do not need to write in detail about the various changes to the divorce laws. You should just be aware that there have been several changes, which have resulted in a more equitable treatment of men and women and have largely done away with the idea that there must be a 'guilty partner'.

> **Exam tip**
> Be aware that it is often difficult to find a single cause for changes in society – show that you realise that the reasons for changes in attitudes or behaviour are usually complex.

Rather than looking at the *number* of divorces, it is more useful to look at the divorce *rate*, which is the number of divorces per 1,000 married people per year. Overall, the divorce rate has slowed down, but it tends to rise in times of economic recession.

If current trends continue, around four out of ten marriages taking place will end in divorce, almost half within the first ten years of marriage. Same-sex marriages have only just become legal, but provisions have been made for divorce, including the grounds of 'unreasonable behaviour'.

Couples may separate, either legally or informally, instead of, or prior to, a divorce. The 2011 Census found that almost 4% of the married population were not living together as a married couple.

> **Exam tip**
> Make quite sure that you understand the difference between a number and a rate.

Child-bearing and the life course

While the decision to have a child is obviously a personal one, the number of children per family, the average age of mothers and so on are governed by social and cultural factors.

An important statistic when looking at child-bearing is the total fertility rate (TFR). This is the average number of children born to a woman over her lifetime. After steadily falling from the high levels in Victorian times (apart from the 'baby booms' of the mid-1940s and 1960s), the 2011 Census showed that the TFR for England and Wales had risen by 18% over the previous decade and stood at 1.9. The increase was put down largely to improvements in fertility treatment and the growing number of first-generation immigrant mothers, coming from societies where the norm for family size was higher than in the UK. However, by 2013 the number of live births had fallen by 4.3%, giving a TFR of 1.8. Reasons for the fall are suggested as:

- changes to the benefits system
- uncertainty over employment in the economic recession
- shortage of affordable housing
- growing costs of raising a child

Another trend in child-bearing is the rise in the average age of mothers, which in 2014 was 30 for the first time. Suggested reasons for this rise include:

- more women participating in higher education and going on to establish a career
- improvements in fertility treatment

Linked to these changes is the fact that around 4% of all UK births are now to women aged 40 and over.

At the other end of the age range, births to teenagers aged 15–19 have fallen. Globally, pregnancies and births to adolescents are seen as a major contributor to **maternal and child mortality** and the cycle of poverty and ill-health, not through biological factors (though these can be important) but because of the socio-economic factors involved, such as interrupted education and difficulties in engaging in the labour market. In 2012, the UK birth rate for females aged 15–19 was 19.7 per 1000. This showed a fall of more than a quarter since 2004, when the rate was 26.9. It is suggested that reasons for the fall do not include the provision of reliable contraception, which has been available for some time, but are more likely to include the following:

- programmes of sex and relationship education in schools
- targeted support for those deemed most at risk
- rising aspirations among many teenage girls

> **Exam tip**
> Remember that there are differences among social and ethnic groups. Teenage births, for example, are more common among working-class than middle-class females, while older mothers are more likely to be found among the middle classes. Pointing out these differences shows good and accurate knowledge.

> **Exam tip**
> The statistics are given to indicate the actual changes. You do not need to memorise them all in detail, but should be able to discuss the trends that they represent, together with some suggested reasons for these.

> **Knowledge check 9**
> What is the difference in meaning between the crude birth rate and the total fertility rate?

> **Maternal and child mortality** The death of the mother and/or child during childbirth or shortly afterwards.

Over the course of a person's life, they are likely to be part of different households and to play different roles. For example, most people start as a child in a nuclear or extended family, some will go on to live with a lone parent, then perhaps to live alone or share a flat with friends or fellow students or workers, then start up their own household, perhaps have children, then possibly live alone again after the breakdown of a relationship, perhaps be part of a reconstituted family, then as the children grow up and leave, live in an 'empty nest' household, then possibly end up living alone again following the death of a spouse or partner.

Family and household structures

Contemporary Britain is characterised by a large variety of **family** types and **household** structures. Class, ethnicity and age all exert an influence and result in differences between groups, but there are some visible trends over the population as a whole.

Much of the information about family and household types comes from the Census, the latest of which was in 2011, which also allows comparison with data from earlier Censuses.

Households

In 2011, there were approximately 25.5 million households in the UK, an increase of 1.6 million since 2001.

Compared with 1961, a smaller proportion of households contain children, and those with children contain fewer children. The average household size decreased from 3.1 people in 1961 to 2.4 people in 2011.

More than 7.5 million people lived alone in 2011. One-person households counted for about 30% of all households. In 1961, the proportion was 12%. However, the age profile of those living alone has changed. Although a significant proportion of them are elderly people, the biggest growth has been among those aged 45–64, a rise of over 36% since 2001. Almost 2.5 million people in this age group live alone.

However, 'living alone' does not necessarily mean not being in a relationship. Research has found that more than one in five people classified as single are actually in a relationship – this represents around 5 million people, or around 9% of adults in Britain. A term has been coined for such people: 'LATs', or 'living apart together'. The increase in LATs is partly contributable to the fact that women no longer need to be living with a man in order to pay bills, have a mortgage, etc.

Families

There were almost 18 million families in 2011, representing 50.7 million people. The most common family type was a married couple, with or without children. The most common family with children contained only one child, making up over 46% of all families with children.

Family Defined by marriage, civil partnership or cohabitation or the presence of children in the household.

Household Defined as a person living alone or a group of people who live and eat at least one meal a day together.

Cohabiting couples, with or without children, accounted for 16% of all families, a rise from 12.5% in 2001. A similar increase was shown in the number of lone-parent families, which accounted for 16.1% of all families in 2011, a rise from 14.8% in 2001.

There has also been a sharp rise in the number of young adults who are living at home with their parents. In 2013, more than 3 million young people aged 20–34 were doing this, representing over a quarter of those in this age group. Some had left home to go to university, but financial pressures meant that they were unable to buy or rent a home of their own so they had returned to live with their parents. This leaving and coming home again has led some to refer to this group as the 'boomerang generation'. Their financial pressures arise from:

■ the increasing difficulty for first-time buyers to obtain a mortgage
■ rising rents, especially in towns and cities
■ high unemployment among young people
■ paying off student loans

Family types

Sociologists have identified a number of family types and it is important to know what these are.

Nuclear family

This is the basic family structure, consisting of two adults and their offspring. It is sometimes called the isolated nuclear family, referring to its self-contained status. Geographical mobility has led to many nuclear families living at a considerable distance from their wider kin.

Extended family

This is where the family has been extended beyond the nuclear family. This can be in the form of a vertically extended family, consisting of three or more generations living together or in close proximity, or a horizontally extended family, for example a household that includes two adult siblings and their families. Taking into account the degree of contact between families, sociologist Peter Willmott has suggested that there are different types of extended family:

■ *Modified extended family*: this is where family members may not live near to or see each other often but maintain regular contact. This has been made easier with the advent of personal computers and social media.
■ *Local extended family*: this is where family members live in fairly close proximity to each other, have regular face-to-face contact, and provide assistance to each other, for example grandparents looking after their grandchildren, or adult children providing practical help to their ageing parents. With more than 80% of parents in work, it has been calculated that grandparents provide around 1.7 billion hours of childcare per year, much of it unpaid.
■ *Dispersed extended family*: this refers to families that do not have regular or frequent contact with each other.

Knowledge check 10

Give two reasons to explain the rise in single-person households among the 45–64 age group.

Reconstituted family

(Also known as a step-family.) This refers to a family in which at least one of the adults has a child or children from a previous relationship living with them and their new partner. The relatively high degree of family breakdown means that reconstituted families are increasingly common. In 2011, almost one in ten children aged 16 and under lived in a step-family.

Kinship carer family

This is a family in which children are being raised by family members other than parents, either because their parents (or the parent that was looking after them) are dead or they are unable to care for them because of issues such as alcohol or drug abuse or mental health problems. The 2011 Census showed that about 173,000 children were living in this type of family. The majority of kinship carers are grandparents, but more than a third of children in this situation were being raised by a sibling. Most kinship care is provided by a single female carer, and more than 90% of kinship care arrangements are informal and fall outside the child welfare system.

Beanpole family

This concept refers to the fact that increased life expectancy means that families now tend to exist over three or more generations, but each generation has fewer children. Drawing a family tree of such a group would look like a beanpole, with a long 'stem' but not many horizontal branches.

Empty-nest family

This is where the adult children have left home. As noted earlier, the rise of the 'boomerang generation' means that many children now return to 'the nest'. In 2013 a quarter of all over-50s had children over the age of 18 living with them.

Evaluation

+ Draws attention to the significant number of changes that have occurred to family and household structures.
+ Recognises the wide variety of family and household types.
+ Shows that social, cultural and economic factors help to shape both family and household structures.
+ Shows that marriage remains an important institution.

Key concepts

monogamy; serial monogamy; cohabitation; civil partnerships; same-sex marriage; divorce; separation; total fertility rate; household; lone-parent family; reconstituted family

Exam tip

While it is important that you know the different types of family and can refer to them as appropriate in exam answers, there is no need to give the full definition (unless this is what the question is asking for). The examiner will know what you mean.

Research exercise

This section could be further researched by carrying out an internet search on certain aspects. Typically, this will give you quantitative data. Typing one of the phrases below (or one of your own choice) is likely to give you a range of possible sources. You need to look carefully at these, as some will be from statistical data, official or otherwise, some will be research abstracts, while others are likely to send you to articles in newspapers or on news websites. Unless you specifically want to widen your search, make sure that the information relates to the United Kingdom or some part of it.

You should not spend too much time on this, but it will allow you to see the variety of resources available and also will give you a little more information on whichever concept you have chosen. Hopefully you will get the opportunity to make reference to your wider knowledge in an exam question – but make sure that the information is relevant.

Suggested concepts are:
- civil partnerships and marriage among same-sex couples
- trends in the divorce rate
- average age of mothers
- teenage pregnancies
- one-person households
- 'LATs' (living apart together)
- boomerang generation
- reconstituted families

Summary

- Marriage is a social institution, governed by both laws and customs.
- Despite the rise in cohabitation and singletons, marriage remains an important institution.
- The norms surrounding marriage have undergone significant changes since the end of the Second World War. It is now more socially acceptable than it was to cohabit and to have children outside of marriage. It is also more socially acceptable, and easier, to get a divorce.
- The laws governing marriage have changed, allowing same-sex couples in England and Wales to marry.
- Most cohabiting couples go on to marry.
- The divorce rate has slowed down, but four out of ten couples now marrying are likely to divorce.
- Family and household structures have changed, reflecting different social norms about marriage, divorce, remarriage and non-marriage, and also changes in family size and increased life expectancy.
- The average age of mothers has risen, largely due to female career opportunities, female participation in higher education, improvements in fertility treatment and women embarking on new relationships following separation or divorce.
- There has been an increase in reconstituted families.
- A growing number of couples who are in a relationship choose not to live together.
- The development of the internet and social media has made it easier for extended family members to keep in contact with each other.

■ Gender roles, domestic labour and power relationships within the family in contemporary society

Gender roles

Gender roles are found in virtually all areas of social life, but are particularly important within the family. As the main unit of primary socialisation, it is within the family that our first experience of gender roles occurs.

Gender roles are the focus of a 'nature/nurture' debate. Are females 'naturally' programmed to be emotional and caring, while males are 'naturally' logical and rational, or are these traits that emerge because of the different ways that many families socialise their children, for example in the toys and games provided (nurture)? Ideas about gender roles are also influenced and propagated by all forms of media output – many situations are shown through the **male gaze**.

One of the main areas of interest in gender roles within the family is that of domestic labour and childcare – which partner does, or is expected to do, what.

There are different perspectives on gender roles within the family.

Functionalist views

Functionalists such as Parsons believed that gendered domestic roles were 'natural' and complementary, and benefited society. Males took the instrumental role and were primarily responsible for being the breadwinner, while females took the expressive and nurturing role and were best suited for domestic work and childcare.

Marxist views

Marxists see the family as a site of exploitation, of both males and females, but particularly of females, whose domestic and child-raising tasks are unpaid labour for the capitalist economy.

Feminist views

Feminists strongly challenge the functionalist view of gendered domestic roles as 'natural'. Oakley's work (1974) on housewives showed that they saw domestic work as dull, repetitive and monotonous, with low status and little job satisfaction. Oakley wrote: 'Women's domesticity is a circle of learnt deprivation and induced **subjugation**: a circle decisively centred on family life' (*Housewife*, 1974). Oakley was saying that whether they like it or not, women's domestic role places on them the burden of housework and childcare. They are 'a slave to housework'. When women do take paid work outside the home, they still assume the main responsibility for domestic and childcare tasks – the 'dual burden'.

Gender roles Reflect the dominant values in society regarding appropriate behaviour and attitudes for males and females.

Male gaze Refers to the habit, particularly among film-makers and news presenters, to show events largely through the eyes of a heterosexual male. Females are often depicted as sex objects, and issues in which females might have a particular interest are dismissed or treated as trivial.

Knowledge check 11

What is meant by 'domestic labour'?

Subjugation To bring someone under your control.

'March of progress' views

Some writers, such as Young and Willmott, believed there was evidence that the 'symmetrical family' was emerging, where household tasks, while still often gendered in nature, were more equitably shared between men and women. It is also argued that the development of new technologies means that even if women are still taking the major share of the work, their tasks have become much easier and less time-consuming.

Domestic labour – the evidence

A very useful source of information is the annual British Social Attitudes (BSA) study. Since 1983 the study has taken a random sample of more than 3,000 UK adults and asked them a series of questions. As many of the questions are repeated each year, it is possible to identify changing trends in people's attitudes towards a range of subjects.

The 30th BSA study, published in 2013, looked at gender roles. Here are some of the main findings, starting with some general points, then moving to the roles of men and women within the family:

- Despite the changes that have occurred in family roles, 'we have not as yet seen a "gender role revolution"'.
- While the 'male breadwinner family system' has been in decline for more than half a century, it is only recently that concerns about 'work–family conflict' have been voiced.
- After 1997 there was an increase in policies designed to encourage mothers, including lone mothers, into the workplace.
- Childcare in the UK remains among the most expensive in Europe, leading to financial burdens for many working parents.
- There has been a clear decline since 1989 in the proportion of people who see women's participation in the labour market as damaging for the family. In 1989, 28% of respondents believed this, but by 2012 only 11% felt that way.
- In 1984, almost half (49%) of respondents supported traditional gender roles. In 2012, the figure had fallen to 13%.
- By 2012 support for the 'traditional division of labour' was much more pronounced among older people and least popular among the youngest age groups.
- In 2012, men on average undertook 8 hours of housework a week. The figure for women was 13 hours.
- In 2012, men on average spent 10 hours a week on care for family members, while women spent 23 hours a week performing these tasks.
- Both some men and some women reported that they felt they were doing 'more than their fair share' of household tasks – 60% of women said this, compared with 10% of men.
- A number of studies have shown that men tend to overestimate the time they spend on household and childcare tasks.

A relatively new gender role that has emerged refers to middle-aged women in their 40s and 50s. They are sometimes referred to as the 'sandwich generation'. This is because they are often 'sandwiched' between looking after adolescent and even adult children (the 'boomerang generation') and the care of their ageing parent or parents. Additionally, many women in this age group are providing often unpaid childcare by looking after their grandchildren while the parents are working.

Exam tip

Remember to mention that both attitudes towards domestic labour and its practice may be affected by social class, ethnicity, religion and age. However, evidence from large-scale studies can illustrate some trends.

Knowledge check 12

What is meant by 'work–family conflict'?

We can therefore conclude that although there have been changes in both attitude and practice with regard to the gendered division of labour, it remains true that women still undertake the major share of household and domestic tasks, even when in paid employment themselves.

Power relationships

Power relationships within the family generally refer to those between the adult partners and between parents and children. By 'power', sociologists are usually referring to the ability of someone to make another person do something, even against their will. While there are examples of the abuse of power within families, such as domestic violence and child abuse, it is more common to be referring to issues of decision-making – who decides where the family will live, how their income is spent, how to bring up the children and so on.

Anthony Giddens (2013) has suggested the emergence of a new relationship ideal, which he calls 'the pure relationship'. This is based on equality and negotiation between the partners. He says that such relationships will last only as long as they continue to offer personal fulfilment to both partners. Critics have cast doubt on the 'equality' aspect and pointed out that the existence of children affects the ability of partners simply to leave the relationship when it is no longer fulfilling.

A similar point about the increasing choice and diversity of relationships leading to the renegotiation of family relationships was made by Beck and Beck-Gernsheim (1995).

Many discussions about power within the family have centred on adult male/female relationships. (Note that there is also relevant material on the role and status of children within the family in the next section on childhood – see p. 31.)

Some research into adult family power relationships has been *microsystemic* – that is, it has looked at how power is shared and exercised within individual families. Other research, particularly by feminist sociologists, has been *macrosystemic*, that is, it has focused on **culturally defined ideologies of gender** within the wider society. It is, of course, possible to combine both approaches by looking at individual families but locating the findings within a wider context.

Some sociologists have drawn attention to the fact that power is not stable within families, that is, no one person always has power over the others, but it should be recognised as a fluid and dynamic process. For example, the male partner might have the main say regarding where the family lives, but decisions about parenting or where and how the children should be schooled might be taken jointly or rest with the mother.

Traditionally, with the pattern of male breadwinner and stay-at-home mother, the male was the main decision-maker. The three factors that conferred greater power to the male were found to be:

- income
- occupational prestige
- educational attainment

Typically, in these traditional family structures, it would be only the male that was bringing income to the household. If the female had an income, it would probably be from a part-time and often low-status 'female' job, thus giving the

Exam tip

This is one area in which it is vital to show that you are aware of significant differences in power relationships within families based on social class, age and, very importantly, ethnicity, where different ethnic groups may have very different cultural ideas and traditions regarding the exercise of power within the family.

Culturally defined ideologies of gender
Sets of ideas referring to the expected roles, behaviours and status of males and females within a particular cultural group, e.g. one based on social class or ethnicity.

male greater occupational prestige. Again, in many families the male would have higher educational attainment, either from schooling or from courses taken and qualifications gained during the course of his employment.

The increasing participation of women in the labour market has in many cases redefined such power relationships, although feminists typically believe that the existence of patriarchy in society still confers greater power on the male.

The abuse of power

In some families, the power of one person over other members of the family is highly abusive in nature. The most common examples are as follows.

Domestic violence

This is typically violence by an adult male against his female partner, but may also include violence against children. There are other forms of domestic violence, such as female violence against a male, or adult or adolescent children against parents, but the male-on-female violence is the most widespread.

- On average, seven women and two men in England and Wales are killed every month by their partner or ex-partner. This figure hasn't changed for 15 years.
- More than 30% of women and 16% of men have experienced domestic abuse at some point since the age of 16.

Despite these shocking statistics, domestic violence is not a specific criminal offence. There are, however, a number of possible offences for which perpetrators can be prosecuted, ranging from murder, rape and manslaughter to assault, harassment and threatening behaviour. However, the absence of a legal definition of domestic violence as a crime leads to problems with the reporting, recording and classifying of incidents by police officers and police forces. Together with the fact that domestic violence is an under-reported offence (it is estimated that fewer than half of incidents are reported to anyone, and possibly only one-fifth are reported to the police) this means that the statistics are not valid and not reliable.

The statistics come from four main sources:

- The Crime Survey for England and Wales – this produces two sets of figures. One set comes from face-to-face interviews asking respondents about their experience as victims. The second comes from confidential self-completion surveys, completed in private using a computer.
- Police data – as domestic violence is not in itself a criminal offence, figures are not published in police crime statistics. However, at police force area level, statistics are collected as 'domestic violence incidence data'. While these are recorded by the Home Office, they are not classified as an official statistic.
- The Crown Prosecution Service – these figures refer to cases brought to court.
- Charities and community organisations – these are able to confirm that the actual extent is greater than the published figures suggest. On average, victims experience 35 incidents of domestic violence before reporting it.

There is no single cause of domestic violence, but it usually occurs in the context of issues of power and control, particularly in the case of male-on-female violence. Many see such actions as rooted in patriarchal traditions that encourage men to believe they are entitled to wield power and control over their partners.

Knowledge check 13

Why might the increasing participation of women in the labour market redefine power relationships within the family?

Knowledge check 14

Identify two reasons why domestic violence is an under-reported crime.

Knowledge check 15

Which set of crime survey figures do you think is the highest, and why?

Forced marriage

A forced marriage is one in which one or both partners do not consent to the marriage. It is not the same as an arranged marriage. Forced marriages occur throughout the world, and there are some groups among which it is a custom take the practice with them when moving to other countries.

In 2005 the British government set up the Forced Marriage Unit to help to prevent the practice and to provide support to victims. In 2013 the unit dealt with more than 1,300 cases – 82% of those involved females and 18% involved males. More than half of victims were under the age of 21 and 1 in 8 was under 16. The cases involved 74 different countries, with almost half relating to Pakistan. From June 2014 forced marriage has been a criminal offence in England and Wales, and parents who force their children to marry can face up to seven years in prison.

Female genital mutilation (FGM)

This practice is widespread in 29 countries in Africa and the Middle East and has been imported by migrants from these countries. FGM is a result of a mixture of cultural, religious and social factors, but at its core is the control of female sexuality. FGM is believed by its practitioners to reduce female sexual desire (libido), thus ensuring pre-marital virginity and marital fidelity. The practice occurs usually between birth and the age of 15, but is most commonly carried out on girls aged between 5 and 8. FGM has been illegal in Britain since 1985, and the crime also covers parents taking their children abroad for the procedure to take place. Up to February 2015 only two prosecutions had been brought in England and both defendants were cleared.

It is thought that some 170,000 women and girls living in Britain have undergone FGM. A report from the Health and Social Care Information Centre in October 2014 identified 467 females who had been newly identified by the NHS as having been the victims of FGM, alongside almost 1,300 who had been identified previously and were being treated. The NSPCC charity reported that there were 23,000 girls under the age of 15 in England and Wales who were at risk.

FGM is an extreme example of the abuse of power that can occur within families.

> **Exam tip**
>
> Always show that you are aware where there are problems with data – as well as knowledge, you can gain marks for evaluation.

Evaluation

- − Functionalists see gendered roles within the family as a positive and natural thing, ignoring the negative consequences for many women.
- − Marxists see women's exploitation as a consequence of capitalism, ignoring other possible causes.
- − Both Marxists and feminists largely see women's roles within the family in a negative way, ignoring the fact that many women enjoy at least some parts of their domestic and childcare tasks.
- + Feminists have drawn attention to the importance of women's roles within the family, an area previously ignored by sociologists.
- + Families are sites of power, with often negative consequences for women and children.

Key concepts

gender roles; conjugal roles; domestic division of labour; nature/nurture debate; instrumental role; expressive role; symmetrical family; domestic violence; forced marriage; female genital mutilation

Knowledge check 16

What is meant by 'conjugal roles'?

Research exercise

This is an opportunity to try out a semi-structured interview to find out about some changes in the family from a female point of view. Your subject should be an older woman – it could be someone from your own family, a friend of the family or, if you are able to obtain appropriate permission, a resident in a local care home. Try to find a suitable person who is at least 70 years old – 80 years old would be even better!

As you will be asking about your respondent's childhood and about her parents, you will be going back quite a long way. If you are able to record the interview (obviously with the respondent's consent), so much the better. If not, you will have to make very brief notes and write it up in a little more detail later.

Aim to spend around 30–45 minutes on the interview. When older people start talking about their childhood they can sometimes speak at great length, so if you aren't able to get through all the suggested topics, don't worry. Suggested questions are given below, but if others occur to you either before or during the interview, just put them in.

Your aim at the end is to have a few paragraphs summarising some changes in family life. If this is a class exercise, you will be able to share your findings with your classmates. Remember that your findings are based on just one person, so will not be representative.

- How old is your respondent? (Don't worry if she doesn't want to state her exact age.)
- How many brothers and sisters did she have?
- How many aunts and uncles did she have? (This will give an idea of how many children were in her parents' families)
- Can she remember her grandparents?
- What kind of toys did she have?
- What games did she play?
- What did her father do for a living?
- Did her mother go out to work? If so, what did she do?
- Can she remember her mother doing the housework? What can she remember? Were there any gadgets or appliances to help?
- Did she ever go on holiday with her family? If so, where?
- At what age did she get married (if she did marry)?
- How many children did she have?
- Did she go out to work?
- How was her life different from her mother's?
- Does she think that family life for women has got better or worse? Why?

Summary

- There is still debate concerning whether gender roles are mainly the result of nature or nurture.
- In many areas of life, there is a difference between the roles and behaviour expected of males and females.
- While there have been some changes in conjugal roles, women continue to take the major responsibility for domestic and childcare tasks.
- Marxists and feminists have drawn attention to the ways in which females are exploited within the family.
- Marxists believe women's exploitation stems largely from capitalism, while feminists see it as a result of patriarchy.
- The family is a site of power, which can be abusive in nature.

The nature of childhood, and changes in the status of children

Childhood is a social construct – that is to say, it is not defined simply by biological age, but is determined by the cultural norms and values of a society. Therefore what we understand by childhood varies by time, by place and by society. In any society, there are often considerable differences both within and between different social class and ethnic groups regarding how long 'childhood' lasts and what is considered appropriate behaviour, knowledge and dress for children.

What do we mean by childhood?

Unlike some societies, in which the end of childhood is marked by a rite of passage, there is no single age in Britain that can be marked as the end of childhood. Rather, childhood ends by degrees, as at various ages the legal right to do certain things (e.g. consent to medical treatment, buy alcohol) is conferred.

There is disagreement regarding whether, in Western societies in general and in the UK in particular, childhood has got 'better' or 'worse' – remember that these are evaluative terms.

'March of progress' views

Those who believe that childhood has got better over time are often referred to as 'march of progress' theorists. Some of the main evidence and arguments they put forward for their views are as follows:

- There has been a significant fall in the **infant mortality rate**. It currently stands at around 4.4 (there are small differences between males and females, with males having a slightly higher rate). Just over 100 years ago, in 1911, the rate was 130.
- Associated with the fall in infant mortality is the fall in the average number of children born per family, as families now can be reasonably confident that their

> **Exam tip**
>
> These are important points and worth stating briefly in any discussion about the changing nature of childhood.

> **Infant mortality rate**
> The number of deaths per year in the first year of life per 1,000 live births.

offspring will survive. This means that more resources per family can be allocated to individual children. These resources are not only material but also include care and affection.

- Children now remain in compulsory education for a long period. Not only does this allow them to increase their knowledge but it keeps them for longer from the necessity to go out and earn a living.
- Increasingly, legislation has prevented children from having to work at a young age and has protected young people when they are at work, e.g. in the hours they can legally work and in the kinds of work that they are allowed to do.
- Children now have a number of legal rights to afford them protection.
- Specialist children's services have been introduced to protect and foster children's health and well-being.
- Research has been carried out into how children's bodies and minds develop, so there is a wealth of information about things such as diet and appropriate play and learning activities.
- There is a huge range of age-appropriate toys and literature available.

Philippe Ariès (1960)

Ariès claimed that the modern view of the family as 'a private domestic circle founded on mutual affection' did not emerge until the seventeenth century. He examined depictions of children in medieval society and one of his most-often quoted statements is: 'In medieval society the *idea* of childhood did not exist.' He argued that children were seen as 'mini adults'.

However, our reading of his text is usually a translation from the original French. Cunningham (1960) points out that the word Ariès used, which has been translated as 'idea', is a French word ('sentiment') that can also mean 'feeling'. Cunningham suggests that what Ariès meant was that in medieval times childhood was not *recognised* and valued as a distinct phase.

Lloyd de Mause (1982)

de Mause claimed that the further back in history one goes, the lower the level of childcare and 'the more likely children are to be killed, abandoned, beaten, terrorised and sexually abused'. In other words, life for Western children had improved.

'Loss of innocence' views

Ideas that childhood in Western societies, including the UK, has got worse over time (particularly in very recent times) are sometimes referred to as the 'loss of innocence' thesis. Those supporting this view offer the following as arguments and evidence:

- Many children now experience the break-up of their parents' relationship. A study by the Marriage Foundation in 2013 found that 45% of teenagers aged 13–15 were not living with both parents. It is argued that relationship breakdown is extremely traumatic for children.
- Despite what we know about the benefits of healthy diets and exercise, a growing number of children have weight problems, either obesity or anorexia.
- Many young people suffer from depression. This can lead to self-harming and, in extreme cases, suicide. It is argued that psychiatric and mental health facilities for young people are woefully inadequate.

Exam tip

Make quite sure that you understand the difference between 'arguments' and 'evidence'. In an exam, questions sometimes ask you to discuss the 'arguments and evidence' for something and you will lose marks if you fail to address both.

Exam tip

If you were able to refer briefly to Cunningham's suggestion in an appropriate context, you would be showing both knowledge and evaluation.

- Children are under increasing pressure to succeed. Published school league tables have contributed to this and it is now commonplace for primary school children to be given regular homework. At the other end of the age range, young people are affected by high unemployment rates for their age group.
- The dividing line between childhood and adulthood is increasingly blurred. Through the internet, social media and the ability to download films and television programmes at any time, children are increasingly exposed to what many would consider highly inappropriate material. As many children have computers with internet access in their bedroom, parents are often unable to control what their children are watching.
- The rise of social media sites has led to incidences of 'cyber-bullying' and pressures on young people to post inappropriate pictures of themselves, which are sometimes then shared online.
- Children are the objects of high-powered consumer campaigns. At a younger age this can lead to 'pester power' when they beg their parents to buy them particular goods, and at older ages young people can be under pressure to achieve a particular body shape and wear certain types of clothing and make-up.

Neil Postman (1982)

Postman believes that both the origin of childhood and the reasons for its decline lie in changes in communications technology. With the advent of the printed word, the passing on of culture no longer relied on oral traditions and literacy became the great divide. Adults could now control the information passed to children. This monopoly and control of information began to crumble with the advent of electronic information, particularly television. Postman argued that television is a visual medium requiring no training to understand, which can be viewed by all. Children are thus exposed to all aspects of the adult world. Postman's ideas could be developed further with the advent and increase of other new forms of communication, including social media and internet sites.

Sue Palmer (2006)

Palmer is not a sociologist but a former head teacher and literacy expert. She looked at a range of problems affecting children – obesity, ADHD, depression, autism, etc. – and argues that while new technologies are benefiting adults, changes in adult lifestyles have affected the way that children are looked after, both at home and at school. She says children's experiences are being 'polluted', leading to 'toxic childhood syndrome'.

Evaluation

- + 'March of progress' (MoP) views demonstrate many positive improvements in the life of children.
- + 'Loss of innocence' (LoI) views draw attention to many contemporary problems affecting children and young people.
- − MoP ignores current problems such as child poverty, child abuse and exploitation.
- − MoP fails to recognise that many children in the past were cherished and cared for.
- − LoI has a romanticised view of childhood in the past.

Child carers

A group of children seldom talked about are those who are carers, looking after a disabled parent or sibling. A report in 2013 from the Office for National Statistics revealed that almost 250,000 children and young people under 19 are carers – about 23,000 of them below the age of 9. Girls are more likely than boys to be carers, and their caring responsibilities have a significant effect on their education. They frequently miss school or are unable to keep up with homework, and their GCSE achievements are significantly lower than average. Those aged 16–19 are more likely to be NEETs (not in education, employment or training) than the average. From April 2015, measures were introduced in the Care Act and the Children and Families Act which say that local authorities must take reasonable steps to identify young carers and assess their needs.

Social and cultural differences

Some research into styles of parenting among different groups has focused on ethnicity. The Swann Report of 1985, for example, attributed the relative underachievement of black (Afro-Caribbean) boys to the fact that many were being raised in lone-parent families with no male role model. Critics pointed out that there was already concern surrounding low levels of achievement among pupils of Bangladeshi origin, most of whom lived in two-parent families.

Further research has indicated that sweeping generalisations about parenting (and indeed other areas) and ethnic group are unhelpful, as differences within ethnic groups are now as important as those between them. However, bearing that important factor in mind, there are some general points that can be made about different groups within the UK.

Chinese parents

Chinese–American mother Amy Chua caused controversy with her book *Battle Hymn of the Tiger Mother* (2011) in which she discussed her child-rearing practices with her two daughters, which included an insistence that they never got a grade less than an A or never failed to come first in any subject except gym and drama. Her book gave rise to the concept of 'tiger moms', that is, parents who are exceptionally ambitious for their children and demand the highest standards from them.

While Chua may have been atypical in her approach, research into Chinese families living in Western societies has found some differences between these families and those of the host country. Stemming largely from their Confucian beliefs, Chinese parents place greater emphasis on obedience, good behaviour, moral training and the acceptance of social obligations, rather than the development of independence, assertiveness and creativity.

Muslim parents

One problem for many British Muslim parents is how to reconcile Western life and values with their Islamic religious ideas and principles. They may therefore be stricter with their children than other groups about such things as attending religious services and aspects of diet and dress. There is a tendency for parents to be stricter with their daughters than their sons over some of these issues.

Social class

Annette Lareau (2003) found in her research among white and black families in the US that class differences in parenting were more important than ethnic group where educational performance was concerned. She dubbed middle-class parenting as 'concerted cultivation'. Middle-class parents involved their children in high levels of extra-curricular activities, some of which were very costly. Working-class parenting was labelled 'accomplishment of natural growth', which meant that working-class parents gave their children more leisure time that was self-directed and unstructured, leaving the children to devise their own games and activities. These class differences cut across ethnic lines. The effect of middle-class parenting was to provide the children with the skills to remain in the middle class. These ideas are similar to those of Bourdieu when he talks about 'cultural capital'.

Children's rights

In 1989, a number of governments around the world signed up to the United Nations Convention on the Rights of the Child. By 'child' is meant here everyone under the age of 18. The Convention has 54 articles, which together set out the civil, political, economic, social and cultural rights that all children are entitled to. You can see a summary of all the articles at www.tinyurl.com/omp4gnu.

Here is a list of some important ones showing the areas covered and the things that governments should ensure:

Article 12	Respect for the views of the child
Article 14	Freedom of thought, belief and religion
Article 16	Right to privacy
Article 19	Protection from violence, abuse and neglect
Article 27	Adequate standard of living
Article 28	Right to education
Article 32	Child labour – protection from economic exploitation and work that is dangerous or harmful
Article 40	Juvenile justice

Office of the Children's Commissioner

This was created under the Children Act of 2004. The role of the Children's Commissioner is to promote and protect children's rights.

Where children's rights are abused

Despite the legislation designed to protect children, there are many examples of children who fail to receive protection. These situations include the following.

Poverty

Many children in the UK are being brought up in poverty. The largest single group of people in poverty are families with children. The Joseph Rowntree Foundation estimates that if current trends continue, by 2020 32% of children, representing more than 3.5 million children, will be living in poverty.

Child trafficking

Many children are trafficked to the UK from abroad, but some are UK citizens moved from one part of the country to another. Trafficking is a *hidden crime* and prosecutions are rare.

The main reasons children are trafficked are:

- sexual abuse
- benefit fraud
- forced marriage
- domestic servitude
- forced labour (e.g. in agriculture or 'sweat shops')
- criminal activities (e.g. for pickpocketing, begging, transporting drugs)

Child abuse

The NSPCC claims that as many as 1 in 20 children has been sexually abused, and of those abused by an adult, 1 in 3 did not tell anyone. Child abuse is another example of a hidden crime.

The global picture

In many countries, the situation for many children is far worse than it is in the UK. Worldwide, millions of children are being brought up in abject poverty, with no access to adequate health care or education, and at work from a very young age. It is estimated that 215 million children under the age of 18 are at work, often in hazardous conditions, and that 16% of all children aged 5–14 in developing countries are workers. Some children are recruited or forced into armed conflicts as soldiers – as many as 250,000 worldwide, 40% of whom are girls.

Key concepts

childhood; social construct; march of progress views; loss of innocence views; toxic childhood

> **Knowledge check 17**
>
> What is meant by a 'hidden crime'?

> **Exam tip**
>
> If a question asks specifically about the UK, or is obviously about the situation in the UK, you must focus your answer on that. However, there may be opportunities to demonstrate that you are aware of the wider, global picture with regard to children's rights. You might be able to do this with a brief contrast between the UK and the global picture.

Summary

- 'Childhood' is a social construct and its meaning varies according to time and place, and also within and between different groups.
- There are two main views about changes in childhood in Britain.
- The 'march of progress' view is that childhood has improved.
- The 'loss of innocence' view is that life has become more difficult for children.
- There are differences in the ways that parents from different groups bring up their children, but social class seems to exert a greater influence than ethnicity.
- Children now have a significant number of legal rights, but there are many cases of the abuse or denial of these rights.

■ Demographic trends in the UK since 1900

'Demography' is the study of populations and demographic trends are changes in those things that affect the composition of a population. These include birth and death rates, how long people are expected to live, the proportion of males and females, and migration both into and out of the country.

The relationship between birth rates and death rates has an important effect on both the size of a population and its age profile. The American demographer Warren Thompson (1929) suggested that populations typically go through four main stages. He called this process **demographic transition**.

- Stage One is characterised by high death rates and high birth rates, with death rates particularly high in the first ten years of life. Population growth is slow, as the high birth rates are counterbalanced by the high death rates.
- Stage Two has falling death rates, particularly among children, but still has high birth rates. This leads to population growth, with a younger age profile.
- Stage Three is characterised by both low death rates and low birth rates. This results in a stable population size.
- Stage Four, which is typical of modern Western societies, has low death rates and very low fertility rates, falling below the rate needed to reproduce the population. This results in an ageing population and a falling population in terms of numbers.

Birth rates

The birth rates in a population are influenced by many things, including the number of women of child-bearing age. Overall, UK birth rates have fallen steadily since 1900. Exceptions are the two 'baby booms' after each of the two World Wars, the one in the 1960s and an 'echo' in the 1980s as the children of the 1960s' boom reached child-bearing age. The fall in the birth rate in 2013 was the largest annual decrease since 1975.

Changes in social norms are reflected in the fact that almost half (47.4%) of births now occur outside marriage or a civil partnership, with just over half (52.6%) taking place within marriage or civil partnership. Reflecting another change in the population is the fact that over a quarter (26.5%) of births are now to women born outside the UK.

Measuring birth rates

One measure of the births occurring in a society is the **crude birth rate** (CBR). The CBR for 2014 was estimated at 12.22; in 1900, it was 26. However, this measure of births in a population is 'crude' in that it measures the number of live births per thousand of all the people in a population, including men, children and women past child-bearing age.

> **Exam tip**
> You will not be expected to remember all the exact figures where rates, etc. are concerned (though it is good if you can remember some of the most important ones), but you must be aware of the overall trends, together with the suggested reasons for changes.

> **Demographic transition**
> The gradual change in a population from one with high death and high birth rates to one with low death and low birth rates. The model was developed to show how the population changes from a pre-industrial to an industrial society.

> **Exam tip**
> Be sure to make clear which rate you are talking about.

> **Crude birth rate**
> The number of live births per thousand of the total population in a given year.

A more satisfactory measure is the **fertility rate**. Yet another measure is the **total fertility rate**. In 2012, the UK total fertility rate was 1.94, and by 2013 it was 1.85. The total fertility rate also gives us another measure, the CFS – completed family size.

Reasons for the fall in birth rates

- *The rising age of mothers.* The older a woman is before she has her first child, the fewer children she is likely to have. Older mothers also find it more difficult to conceive.
- *The survival of children.* In 1900, before the welfare state, poorer families especially needed to have some surviving children to care for ageing parents. As more children survived, the need to have as many offspring fell.
- *Economic cost.* Children used to be an economic asset for their family, earning wages from a very early age. As the age of compulsory education has risen, children are increasingly an economic cost, making it more difficult for families to support large numbers of children. Figures published in 2015 by the Centre for Economics and Business Research show the cost of raising a child to the age of 21 has risen by 63% since 2003 and stands at about £230,000 per child, with the first four years of life being the most expensive.
- *Improved availability and reliability of contraception.* The contraceptive pill was made available on the NHS in 1961, though initially only to married women who had already borne children. In 1974, it was made available on prescription to single women.
- *Legalised abortion.* Women have always resorted to abortion, often at devastating cost to themselves. From 1967, under certain conditions, abortion was made legal in England, Wales and Scotland, though not in Northern Ireland. (In Northern Ireland, currently abortion is permitted only where there is a direct threat to the mother's life, though in February 2015 a judicial review was announced, to see whether this could be widened to take in cases of rape, incest or fatal foetal abnormalities.)
- *Women's increased participation in the labour market.* While many mothers are in paid employment, this is obviously more difficult with larger families.
- *The growing number of women who remain childless.* Of women born in 1968 (i.e. whose child-bearing years are thought to be over), 18% are childless, compared with 11% of women born in 1941.

Death rates

The deaths in a population are measured by the **crude death rate**, sometimes referred to as the mortality rate. This is affected by the **age distribution of the population**. The current UK death rate is 9.34; in 1900 it was around 16. The term 'mortality rate' is usually applied when the deaths among a particular section of the population are being measured, such as among infants, women in childbirth, or people in specific age groups.

Fertility rate
The number of live births per thousand women of child-bearing age in a given year. For demographic purposes, the child-bearing period is reckoned as ages 15–44.

Total fertility rate
The number of children a woman in a given population is likely to have by the end of her child-bearing years, based on the current birth rates in that population.

Exam tip

As with many other demographic trends, show that you are aware that the overall figures disguise differences between groups, particularly differences in social class, ethnic group and religion.

Crude death rate
The number of deaths per thousand of the population in a given year.

Age distribution of the population
The proportion of people in different age groups throughout the population.

The largest fall in death rates since 1900 has been among infants and children. Death rates among this group fell to low levels by 1950. Adult death rates fell more slowly. The greatest fall in mortality among people of advanced ages has occurred since the 1970s.

In 1900, more than 50% of all deaths were of those under the age of 45. In 1911, 63% of people died before the age of 60. The current rate for the under-60s is around 12%.

While in the early twentieth century infectious diseases were one of the main causes of death, the greatest causes of mortality are now heart disease, cancer, strokes, dementia/Alzheimer's disease and accidents. Partly these causes reflect an ageing population.

Death rates vary by social class, with higher rates of premature death among the working class.

Infant mortality rate (IMR)

This measures the number of babies who die before their first birthday per thousand live births in a given year. The IMR is often used as a general measure of the health of a population. In the UK, it has been falling steadily since 1900, though there were increases in the depression of the 1920s and 1930s, and during the Second World War. The rate now stands at 4.44, whereas in 1900 it was 140. Half of all babies who died in 1900 did so as a result of infectious diseases such as measles, whooping cough and diphtheria.

However, while the overall IMR has been falling, there are still sharp differences between the social classes, with infant deaths 35% more common among those from manual than those from non-manual backgrounds.

> **Exam tip**
>
> Show that you know that the IMR is one measure that shows a clear difference between social classes.

Reasons for the fall in death rates

- Advances in medicine, both in diagnosis and treatment, with particular advances in surgery.
- Significant improvements in public health, sanitation, housing and the supply of clean water.
- Programmes of vaccination, which have had a particularly beneficial effect on infants and children, and helped significantly to reduce death rates from infectious diseases.
- The introduction of the National Health Service in 1947, providing free treatment and care.
- The development of antibiotics.
- Improvements in ante-natal and post-natal care.
- Improved food production and a generally higher standard of living.
- Changes in the law resulting in safer working conditions, though there are still some occupations that are particularly hazardous.

Family size

Family size is obviously important, as children represent the next generation of the population. As we have seen, the average number of children born to women has been falling steadily, apart from a few 'baby booms'. The 2011 Census showed that the most common family with children contained only one child, making up 46% of all families with children.

An important concept in demography is **replacement fertility**. If we ignore the effects of migration, we might assume that to keep the population from falling, each couple should have two children, thus replacing themselves. However, because not everyone survives to have children, because more males than females are born, and because not all women will have children, replacement fertility needs to be slightly more than two children per couple.

While there have been more births than deaths each year in the UK every year since 1975, this has largely been the effect of increased life expectancy. In fact, fertility has fallen below replacement level in England, Wales and Scotland since the early 1970s. Northern Ireland did not fall below replacement level until 1993.

Inward migration can have an effect on replacement fertility. This is because migrants tend to be younger people, and some coming to the UK are from countries where typical family sizes are larger than the UK norm. However, migrants still form only a small part of the UK population, so the current impact on fertility levels is small.

There are two main effects of below replacement fertility levels, namely an ageing population and overall population decline. The twin effects of low fertility rates and increased life expectancy mean that the proportion of the total population in the older age groups rises. This has an effect on the **dependency ratio**. This means that the earnings of each person of working age have to support an increased number of dependants. Equally, over time, the overall size of the population will fall.

There are two exceptions to the general rule of falling family size.

Muslim families

The 2011 Census found that although Muslims accounted for 4.8% of the UK population, 9.1% of children up to the age of four were Muslim, and Muslim families typically contain more children than the average non-Muslim family. However, there are three important points to be made here.

First, the Census question asking for religious affiliation was optional and 7% of the population did not answer. In fact, there were more children aged 0–4 in the 'religion not stated' category than Muslim children.

Second, the age profile of the Muslim population is different from that of indigenous groups. Almost half of Muslims in Britain are under the age of 25 and 88% are under 50. This means that they have a much higher proportion of people of child-bearing age than the wider population. Muslims showed the youngest age profile of all religious groups.

Third, we should look at Muslim families in a global context. Around the world, the average Muslim family fell from one with 4.3 children in 1995 to one with 2.9 children in 2010. Muslim families are expected to converge with Western family sizes by the mid-twenty-first century.

Quiverfull families

'Quiverfulls' belong to a Christian evangelical movement whose followers do not use contraception and who believe that it is their Christian duty to have as many children as

Replacement fertility
The level of fertility required to ensure that a population reproduces itself in size.

Knowledge check 18

Why might Northern Ireland be different from the rest of the UK in this respect?

Dependency ratio
The percentage of dependent people (those not of working age, i.e. 0–15 and 65-plus) to the percentage of people of working age.

possible. The name comes from Psalm 127, in which children are compared to arrows for use in war, and which contains the line 'Blessed is the man whose quiver is full of them'. The movement started in the US and has spread to the UK, but the number of followers is currently so small that it fails to have any impact on average family size.

Reasons for the change in family size

Couples are delaying having their first child, meaning that the potential child-bearing period is shortened.

The economic cost of raising a child means that many couples delay having a second child or decide to have only one child.

Women's greater participation in the labour market contributes both to the delay in starting a family and to the decision to limit the number of children, due to the difficulties of being a working parent.

Exam tip

Again, remember the variations in family size among different social class, religious and ethnic groups.

Life expectancy and an ageing population

There has been a more or less continuous rise in **life expectancy** since 1900. In 1900, life expectancy at birth was 47 for males and 50 for females. Half of all deaths occurred in those under 45. At the time of writing, life expectancy is 80.42 — 78.26 for males and 82.69 for females. There are currently around 8 million people in the UK expected to live to at least 100. Between 2010 and 2030, the number of over 65s and the number of over 85s in the population are both expected to increase by more than 50%. It is estimated that around a third of babies born today will survive to their 100th birthday.

Increased life expectancy, when combined with low fertility rates, leads to an ageing population. This has important consequences for society as a whole.

Life expectancy The average age to which people are expected to live. Life expectancy can be measured at any age – for example at birth, at the start of adulthood and at the start of old age.

- *Welfare payments* – as more people will be drawing their pensions and may also be in need of other benefits, this will increase the welfare bill.
- *Retirement age* – partly in order to fund this, the age at which people can retire from work and draw a pension will rise.
- *Health and social care* – older people increasingly have various health conditions and need medication and hospital care more frequently than younger people. This will put a strain on the NHS and social services.
- *Accommodation* – there will be a growing need for places in care homes and assisted living facilities for those unable to look after themselves. There will also be a demand for suitable housing, e.g. single-storey specially adapted houses.
- *Family carers* – at least in the initial stages of a person's physical and/or mental decline, family members provide at least some care. The number of those caring for elderly relatives will increase.
- *Crime rate* – as older people are less likely than younger ones to commit crime, the overall crime rate could fall.
- *Politics* – older people tend to have a higher voting turn-out rate than younger people, which might have an effect on the policies that parties offer.
- *Support* – by no means all older people need care and support. Many of them provide invaluable help to younger members of their family, e.g. in childcare and financial support.

Knowledge check 19

What is meant by 'an ageing population'?

Reasons for the increase in life expectancy

There is no single reason for the steady increase in life expectancy, but the following have all been contributory factors:

- advances in medicine, especially in surgery and the control of infectious diseases
- improvements in sanitation and housing
- improvements in food supply and quality
- the introduction of the welfare state and the National Health Service
- new drugs to cure or to extend the life of those with once-fatal diseases, such as some types of cancer
- the decline in the number of people smoking
- improvements in health education and preventive medicine, giving people the knowledge to live a healthy lifestyle

Exam tip

Remember that there are social class differences in life expectancy.

Migration and globalisation

Migration

Migration refers to the flow of people in and out of a country, usually measured in thousands per year. Immigration refers to the number of people coming into a country to live and work, while emigration refers to those leaving a country. The difference between these two figures is known as net migration. Net migration figures are important as they give an idea about changes in population size. If more people are entering a country than leaving, the population is likely to grow over time, especially if the migrants are younger people of child-bearing age. Conversely, if more people are leaving than entering a country, the population is likely to decline. Currently, England, Scotland and Wales are countries of net immigration, while Northern Ireland is a country of net emigration.

Concerns among some groups about the level of immigration of foreign-born people and its effect on the economic and cultural life of the UK have meant that immigration has become an important political issue.

Exam tip

Always remember when asked about 'migration' that it refers to both immigrants and emigrants.

Demographic impact of migration

The number of births in a population is obviously one important factor affecting population size. The number of births in a given period is determined by both the size and age structure of the female population and fertility rates. Populations are likely to grow if there is a high proportion of foreign-born female immigrants of child-bearing age, and if fertility rates in the country of origin are higher than in the host country. Both of these factors occur in UK immigration patterns, thus contributing to population growth.

Predicting future patterns of population change is obviously difficult, but it is estimated that if current migration trends continue, the cumulative effect of post-2012 migrants will account for 43% of the total UK population increase until 2037. Scotland presents an interesting picture, as without net migration (i.e. more immigrants than emigrants) its population would stagnate for the next two decades and would then decline.

Who are the migrants?

A significant group, both as immigrants and emigrants, are Poles. Even a poorly paid job in the UK pays more than most Poles can earn at home, so many Poles come to work in the UK. Many stay for only a limited period and then return to Poland, thus becoming emigrants. Poles represent the second-largest number of foreign citizens living in the UK. However, when measuring migrants by country of birth rather than nationality, the Indian community remains the largest. This is because many more Indians than those from other nationalities take British citizenship. The most common countries of birth of foreign-born residents in the UK are India, Poland, Ireland and Pakistan. UK-born people also figure among the immigrants, as those who have moved to live or work abroad return home.

Around 7 million people out of a UK population of about 64 million are foreign-born, with London having the greatest proportion of immigrants.

Why do people come to the UK?

Apart from British-born citizens returning home after living abroad, the most common reasons for people coming to the UK are as follows:

- *Work* – in 2013, foreign-born workers made up just over 9% of those in work. The growth was fastest in relatively low-skilled occupations. While females used to outnumber males, there is now an even gender distribution.
- *Study* – a very large number of foreign-born young people come to the UK to study, but their stay is almost always temporary. Around 18% of all students in higher education come from abroad, with China contributing the largest proportion (almost 20%). Foreign students contribute a huge amount to the income of UK universities and to the economy generally. Attitudes towards foreign-born students are considerably less hostile than to members of other immigrant groups.
- *Joining a family member* – the rules have been tightened. Only British citizens or those resident in the UK earning a particular gross annual salary set by the government can apply to allow their spouse, partner, fiancé(e) or child(ren) to enter and live in the UK. In addition, any proposed dependants must demonstrate an intermediate level of English and pass the 'Life in the UK' test.
- *Asylum* – asylum seekers represent only a small proportion of immigrants, as the rules granting them permission to stay are very strict. Applications have increased following the growing number of conflicts around the world. Opinion polls repeatedly show that respondents considerably overestimate the number of asylum seekers in the population. It is in fact very difficult to get asylum and around two-thirds of applications are rejected. Around 23,000 people a year apply for asylum in the UK.

Attitudes towards immigration

Immigration is an important political issue in the UK, regularly featuring as one of the main issues of concern to voters. Although opposition to immigration, or at least further immigration, is quite widespread, research has found that people are generally less hostile to immigration if they actually know and mix with someone from a minority ethnic group. This helps to explain why people living in areas with the least ethnic diversity are the most likely to call for curbs on immigration. Attitudes towards

Exam tip

It is very important to know that people migrate to the UK for different reasons. Make sure that you learn the list of reasons given above.

immigration also vary by age and social class, with younger people showing generally less concern than older people, and those from the higher social classes generally less hostile than those from the working class.

Those who oppose immigration are likely to hold negative perceptions of the impact of migrants on British jobs, crime rates, welfare and public services and culture. There is strong evidence that opposition to immigration occurs when there is a perceived threat to one's group, especially issues concerning national identity or culture.

Explanations of attitudes towards immigration

While this is obviously a complex issue, three basic explanations of attitudes towards immigration have been extensively researched:

- *Contact theory* – more positive attitudes to members of another group occur when there is sustained and positive contact with members of other ethnic, religious or national groups.
- *Group conflict theory* – migrants or minority groups can appear to threaten the interests, identities or status of the majority group, and those who feel this sense of threat are more likely to oppose immigration.
- *Economic competition theories* – opposition to immigration will come from (a) native workers who are competing with immigrant workers with similar skills, and/ or (b) wealthier natives who consider there is a financial burden for tax payers if immigrants use public services such as schools and hospitals.

> **Knowledge check 20**
>
> Suggest two reasons why attitudes towards immigration might vary by age and social class.

> **Knowledge check 21**
>
> State what is meant by 'net migration'.

Globalisation

Globalisation refers to the increasing integration and interdependence of countries and their economies, societies, cultures, politics, technology and ecology. Globalisation has had many effects on the UK. Among the most important are the following:

- *Global markets* – these affect where work is located and where goods and some services are sold. Many UK companies have outsourced some of their work to overseas companies. The manufacture of clothes and shoes, banking and insurance, customer services, the provision of educational materials and even the marking of examinations are all employment sectors that have been at least partially outsourced abroad. This has resulted in many UK employees losing, or becoming fearful of losing, their employment. However, there is often a positive socio-economic effect on the country to which the work is outsourced. There are more opportunities for skilled workers, which in turn has a positive impact on the participation rate in education. Many employment opportunities are created for women, who now form an important part of the labour market in some developing countries. Many UK workers now work for foreign companies and some spend at least part of their time working abroad. The impact of global interconnections was keenly felt following the financial collapse of 2008, with many Western societies imposing austerity measures on their population.
- *Global society* – this refers to the social connections that are made between people via the internet, social media and the relative ease and low cost of foreign travel. At its best, these can introduce new ideas and experiences and result in people having positive experiences in different countries. There is also the 'dark side', featuring issues such as so-called 'sex tourism' and the grooming and trafficking of young people between societies.

- *Global culture* – with the rise of global brands, the same foods and drinks, clothes, toys, games, household and beauty products, even films and TV programmes, are now found throughout the world. Some argue that this leads to a loss of local traditions and practices, replacing them with a unified 'global culture of consumption'.
- *Global governance* – there are now several institutions which have a global or international remit to decide aspects of our lives. Examples include the United Nations, the World Health Organization and the World Bank.

Knowledge check 22

What is meant by 'globalisation'?

Key concepts

demography; crude birth rate; fertility rate; crude death rate; mortality rate; infant mortality rate; replacement fertility; life expectancy; ageing population; migration; globalisation

Summary

- With a few exceptions, birth rates have fallen steadily since 1900.
- A growing proportion of births are now to women born outside the UK.
- The largest fall in death rates occurred among babies and young children. Adult death rates fell more slowly.
- Life expectancy has increased considerably, with the result that the UK has an ageing population.
- The UK is now a country of net inward migration.
- Globalisation has affected many institutions and areas of life.

Methods used to study families and households

It is important when looking at any topic in sociology to know how the evidence has been obtained. A helpful way to revise this is to have a section in your folder headed 'Research methods', with a series of sheets each headed with a particular method. Ideally, you should have a section for every topic that you are studying, but we focus here on families and households.

If you start at or near the beginning of your course, you will build up a useful revision aid. As you come across the various pieces of research, note the method or methods used and enter the author(s) and study title under the appropriate heading. You may even wish to write a sentence or two about the nature and main findings of the research. You may not end up with something for each method for each topic. The following may help you to get started, with just an example or two – you will find a lot more.

Primary data

Interviews

It would be helpful to divide these into structured/semi-structured and unstructured. Examples would be Oakley on 'Housework' and Rapoport and Rapoport on 'Dual career families'.

Exam tip

It is always helpful if you can show that you know how research evidence was gained. You don't necessarily need to go into detail (unless the question asks you specifically about the methods used). A phrase such as 'As Oakley's interviews with housewives in the 1970s showed ...' will usually be sufficient.

Knowledge check 23

What is meant by primary and secondary data?

Observation

A good example would be the observation of children's play by Iona and Peter Opie.

Participant observation

The classic study by Young and Willmott, 'Family and kinship in East London', is a good example of this.

Oral history

Paul Thompson's book *The Edwardians* arose out of his oral history research into family life.

Secondary data

Historical documents

These include diaries, letters, past Censuses, novels and even portraits. The work of Ariès on childhood fits here.

Official statistics

Much of our knowledge of changes to family and household structure, birth and death rates, migration and so on comes from statistical reports, including the Census. The Office for National Statistics is a good place to start.

Longitudinal studies

These are usually a subset of official statistics and provide useful information about changes over time. Good examples are the British Social Attitudes Surveys and Understanding Society.

Non-official statistics

These come from a variety of sources, including charities and 'think tanks'. They are often useful for information on issues such as domestic violence, child sexual abuse and child trafficking as they are usually working with victims, many of whom will not have reported the offences and will therefore not appear in the official statistics.

> **Knowledge check 24**
>
> What is the difference between structured and unstructured interviews?

> **Knowledge check 25**
>
> What is a longitudinal study?

Questions & Answers

How to use this section

In this section you will find three questions at AS and three at A-level. Each has two student answers, one at about an A grade, the other at about a C grade, with comments on the answers throughout. There is an additional practice question at both AS and A-level for you to try, though there are some tips to help to keep you on track.

While the structure and mark allocation of AS and A-level are different, and you should be careful to know exactly what your particular exam will be like, there is no harm in reading through and trying the 'other' questions – indeed, it will serve as good revision.

You should read each question carefully and either try to answer it in full or at least make notes of how you would answer it *before* reading the student answer and comments. This might help to pick up on mistakes you have made or things that you are doing well. Remember that there is no single perfect way of answering an exam question – the highest marks can be gained by taking different approaches, especially in the higher-mark questions. However, the comments should help to show you the kinds of approach that would do well and some of the pitfalls to avoid.

As a general point, you should always read through the whole question before starting to write. When you come to answer the question that is based on an Item, read the Item particularly carefully, as it will contain material that is essential to answering the question.

Examinable skills

AQA sociology examination papers are designed to test certain defined skills. These skills are expressed as assessment objectives (AOs) and are the same for AS and A-level, though the weighting given to each differs between the two levels. There are three AOs and it is important that you know what these are and what you have to be able to do in an exam to show your ability in each. Further guidance on each of the AOs is given in the comments. In practice, many answers to questions, particularly those carrying the higher marks, will contain elements of all three AOs.

Assessment objective 1

Demonstrate knowledge and understanding of:
- **sociological theories, concepts and evidence**
- **sociological research methods.**

Your exam answers will have to demonstrate clearly to the examiners that your knowledge is accurate and appropriate to the topic being discussed and that you have a clear understanding. It is not enough simply to reproduce knowledge learned by rote; you must be able to use this knowledge in a meaningful way to answer the specific question set. This means that you must be able to *select* the appropriate knowledge from everything you know and use only the knowledge that is relevant to, and addresses the issues raised by, the question.

Assessment objective 2

Apply sociological theories, concepts, evidence and research methods to a range of issues.

In certain questions in the exam you will be presented with an Item – a short paragraph setting the context for the question that is to follow, and providing you with some information to help answer it. You *must* take this relevant information and use (apply) it in your answer. However, 'applying' the material does not mean simply copying it from the Item and leaving it to speak for itself. You will need to show your understanding of the material by doing something with it, such as offering a criticism, explaining something about it, linking it to a particular sociological theory or offering another example of what is being stated or suggested. You will therefore be using your own knowledge to add to the information that you have been given and will be *applying* it appropriately to answer the question.

Assessment objective 3

Analyse and evaluate sociological theories, concepts, evidence and research methods in order to:
- **present arguments**
- **make judgements**
- **draw conclusions.**

The skill of *analysis* is shown by breaking something down into its component parts and subjecting those parts to detailed examination. Analysis is shown by providing answers (depending, of course on what it is that you are analysing) to questions such as 'who said or who believes this?', 'what does this concept relate to?', 'what does this research method entail?', 'how was this evidence collected?' and so on. The skill of *evaluation* is shown by the ability to identify the strengths and weaknesses or limitations of any sociological material. It is not sufficient, however, simply to list the strengths or limitations of something – you need to be able to say *why* something is considered a strength or otherwise, and sometimes you will need to state *who* claims that this is a strength or weakness. Depending on what it is you are discussing, you may be able to reach a conclusion about the relative merits or otherwise of something, but remember that any conclusions should be based on the rational arguments and solid sociological evidence that you have presented during your answer.

Weighting of assessment objectives

In the exam papers, each AO is given a particular weighting, which indicates its relative importance to the overall mark gained. The weightings are not the same for AS and A-level, so be sure that you look at the one that is appropriate for the exam you will be taking.

Weighting for AS examinations			
Assessment objective	Paper 1 (approximate %)	Paper 2 (approximate %)	Overall weighting
AO1	22	24	46
AO2	18	13	31
AO3	10	13	23
Overall	50	50	100

Weighting for A-level examinations				
Assessment objective	Paper 1 (approximate %)	Paper 2 (approximate %)	Paper 3 (approximate %)	Overall weighting
AO1	15	13	16	44
AO2	11	11	9	31
AO3	8	9	8	25
Overall	34	33	33	100

Command words

Ofqual, the body that sets the criteria for all GCE sociology specifications, has an approved list of 'command words' used in exam questions. The following are some of the most commonly used, but it is important to remember that the list is not exhaustive and occasionally other, similar, words or phrases may be used instead. All this shows how important it is to take time in an exam and read the questions carefully before you start writing. It is worth learning what is meant by these command words to ensure you give an appropriate response.

- *Define* – give the meaning of something
- *Explain* – give purposes or reasons
- *Outline* – give the main characteristics
- *Outline and explain* – give the main characteristics and develop these
- *Using one example, briefly explain* – use an example to give a brief account of something
- *Analyse* – separate information into components and identify their characteristics
- *Evaluate* – make judgements from the available evidence
- *Applying material from the Item …* – draw on the material provided and develop it using your own knowledge to answer the question

■ The AS examination

The topic of *Families and households* is examined on Paper 2 of the AS examination, 'Research methods and topics in sociology'. The question appears in Section B of Paper 2, as 3.2.2.2, and is one of four options. The whole exam lasts for 1 hour 30 minutes, carries 60 marks and is worth 50% of the AS qualification. Section B questions are worth 40 out of the 60 total marks. You should therefore spend about an hour answering the *Families and households* question, trying to manage your time so that you have time to read through the whole paper at the end.

Question 1

1   Define the term 'domestic division of labour'.   (2 marks)

ⓔ There are two parts to this concept: 'domestic' and 'division of labour'. Make sure you include both in your definition.

2   Using one example, briefly explain how increased life expectancy may affect household structure.   (2 marks)

ⓔ There is no need to define 'increased life expectancy' – your answer should make it clear what you are talking about. Make sure you focus on 'household structure' rather than roles. If you are unsure, you can always include a second example, but this should not be standard practice – extra examples use up time.

3   Outline three reasons for changes in the status of children in society.   (6 marks)

ⓔ Make sure you have three reasons and put each one on a separate line so that the examiner is able to distinguish between them. Remember the question is about 'status', not 'role'.

4   Outline and explain two ways in which the role of fathers has changed over the past 70 years.   (10 marks)

ⓔ Make sure you have two different ways and that your focus is clearly on the role of fathers. While the timescale does not have to be precise, 70 years goes back roughly to the end of the Second World War, so don't spend time talking about fathers in medieval or Victorian times. In this type of question, it is helpful to separate out your explanations, having them in different paragraphs and/or using 'One way is …' and 'A second way is …' to introduce the separate points.

5   Read Item A and answer the question that follows.

> ### Item A
> Research by feminist sociologists such as Oakley showed that gender roles were unequal in many families, with women taking the greatest share of housework and childcare. Some sociologists argued that this was because these roles were 'natural'. However, it is now claimed that there is a growing equality between partners, with domestic tasks being shared more equally.

Applying material from Item A and your knowledge, evaluate the contribution of feminists to our understanding of gender roles within the family.   (20 marks)

e There are three pieces of information in the Item that you should use (apply) in your answer – that research into gender roles was carried out by feminist sociologists and what their research showed, that some claimed that different gender roles are 'natural', and the claim that things have changed. Make sure you use all of these, not simply copying the phrases but discussing them. Your evaluation should look at how and why the research was useful and also consider the arguments and evidence regarding whether and to what extent things have changed.

Student A

1 This refers to how the adult partners in a family divide up the jobs – mainly housework and childcare but also things like DIY and gardening. In other words, who does what.

e **2/2 marks awarded.** A concise and accurate definition.

2 With increased life expectancy, people are living to a much greater age than they used to. Sometimes this means that people are no longer able to look after themselves, especially if they are widowed, so the adult children might take their aged parent to live with them, possibly making an extended family structure with three generations under the same roof.

e **2/2 marks awarded.** This is an appropriate example which is clearly explained. There is no need to define the term, as the student has done in the first sentence.

3 One reason is that children are now dependent for longer, because the age of compulsory education has increased. They have their dependent status for longer than children in Victorian times did, when children could leave school at 11.

A second reason is that as the family size has decreased and most families have only one or two children, each child can have more time and money spent on them, making them seem more precious and important and giving them higher status. This is seen in China with the one-child policy, where children are referred to as 'little emperors'.

A third reason is that children now have many more legal rights than they used to and can be protected by the state. They have a defined legal status whereas in the past they were almost 'non-persons'.

e **6/6 marks awarded.** Three reasons are given and clearly outlined. Beware of writing more than you need to in these short questions – for example, the reference to China was unnecessary.

4   In most families, even beyond the 1950s, fathers were seen as 'the head of the family', someone to be obeyed and who had great authority over his wife and children. Typically, this type of father did not take part in the domestic running of the home, and it was the woman who had responsibility for housework and childcare, while the father's main role was as the breadwinner.

e This is quite a good introduction, as it is setting the scene with a brief look at how a father's role was seen in the past, sticking to the timescale mentioned in the question. It is not essential to write an introduction to this type of question, but if you have the time and keep it brief, it can be useful.

The many changes that have taken place in the family in recent years have had the effect of changing the roles of both mothers and fathers. One way in which the role of fathers has changed is that while mothers used to give up paid work when they had children (in many jobs they were forced to do this), now most mothers are in employment, sometimes part-time but often full-time. **a** This means that fathers are seldom the only breadwinner, and in some families the mother earns more than the father. One result of this is that fathers have to share the decision-making about family finances. This has removed some of their authority over the family. **b** Having a wife at work has also meant that more men take a greater share than they used to in housework and childcare, though the majority of this is still done by the woman. **c** It is no longer unusual, though, to see fathers out pushing baby buggies or playing with their children in the park. Also, most fathers now go to ante-natal classes with their pregnant wife or partner, and will often be at the birth, something that never used to happen. It is now much more acceptable for fathers to show their 'feminine' side. **d**

Another way in which the role of many fathers has changed is as a result of family breakdown. Many fathers no longer live with their children and may not see them very often. It is still the case that courts tend to award custody of children to the mother when there is a divorce or separation. **e** Movements such as Fathers4Justice have emerged to try to make sure that fathers' rights to see their children are upheld. **f** Also, some divorced or separated fathers go into new relationships and may become the 'father' to stepchildren, which can result in difficulties about how much authority they have over them. So many men are not able to play the role of full-time fathers to their own children but may have to take on the role of father to stepchildren. **g**

The role of father though is not the same in all groups. There are class and especially ethnic differences. Some middle-class men work such long hours that they don't see much of their younger children, and in some Asian and/or Muslim groups the father is still very much the authority figure with control over his wife and children, especially daughters.

ⓔ This is a very detailed answer – remember that there are only 10 marks available for this question, so be sure not to spend too much time on it. The two points have been separated out, which is helpful to examiners. In fact, the first section contains more material than is necessary. **ⓐ** The main point is the change in fathers' roles as a result of women taking on paid employment. **ⓑ** This is analysed (broken down) into points about sharing decision-making and a possible loss of authority. **ⓒ** A further point is made about fathers taking more of a share in housework and childcare, with the evaluative point about women still taking the greater share. **ⓓ** The point about fathers being able to show their 'feminine side' is a good one, though it isn't necessary to give as many examples.

The second point is about changes brought about by family breakdown. **ⓔ** The important point is made about the awarding of custody and how this changes fathers' roles. **ⓕ** There is the good example of how some fathers try to maintain links with their children. **ⓖ** A final important point is made about the number of men who play both a father and a stepfather role.

There is then the final evaluative section pointing out that the role of father is not the same in all groups, with a couple of accurate illustrative examples.

Overall, this is a thorough and detailed answer. While it gains top marks, the student has written more than is necessary – it is worthwhile throughout your course to work out roughly how much time is available for the larger-mark questions and to get as much practice as possible in learning how much you can write in the time allowed. **10/10 marks awarded.**

---

5 Although the study of the family has been important in sociology, until fairly recently there was not much research into gender roles. As Item A says, it was thought that domestic and childcare tasks were 'natural' to women. This is what functionalists called the expressive role, and they said it complemented the male 'instrumental' role. **ⓐ**

Oakley's research in the 1970s was one of the first studies into what women actually did in the home and what they thought about it. Using in-depth interviews, she found that women were mainly dissatisfied with the housewife role and found it boring and monotonous. **ⓑ** When Oakley's research was carried out, most married women, at least when they had children, left work and became full-time housewives. Since then, things have changed a lot and most women, even those with children, are in paid employment, sometimes part-time. **ⓒ**

According to the Item, things have now changed and gender roles in the family have become more equal. **ⓓ** However, sociologists, including feminist sociologists, have continued to research domestic roles and many findings do not support this claim. **ⓔ**

Barrett and McIntosh, writing from a Marxist perspective, see housework as unpaid labour that benefits men. Delphy also argues that the housewife role is created by patriarchy. This goes against the functionalist view that doing cooking and cleaning and looking after children is 'natural' for women.

Other feminist sociologists have looked at gender roles, particularly from the woman's point of view. Hochschild looked at how women, even if in paid work, still came home and did the bulk of the chores and housework, and called this the 'second shift'. Duncombe and Marsden went a step further and said that as well as work and housework, etc. women did most of the 'emotion work' in families. They said this was the 'triple shift' undertaken by women. Ansley said that women were the 'shit takers' in families, carrying most of the burden. f

Some of this research is now quite dated, so have things changed? Man-Yee Kan in 2001 found that women still did more housework than men. However, there were differences between families. Educated women did not do as much housework as women with less education, and women with very high earnings also did less. Man-Yee Kan argued that their higher income gave them greater bargaining power within the family. Somerville, a liberal feminist, argues that some progress has been made and gender roles are more equal than they used to be. g However, research carried out for Radio 4's 'Woman's Hour' in 2014 showed that women still did nearly 12 hours a week of housework while men did 6, and the Institute for Public Policy Research found that 8 out of 10 women did more household chores than their partner. h

Hakim criticises feminists for trying to achieve equal gender roles as she says that women have a choice and many women actually choose to take the bigger share of domestic work. i

One of the problems is actually measuring who does what, as it obviously relies on what people say they do – you can't spend time in hundreds of households watching who does what and for how long. Studies have shown that men typically overestimate the time they spend on domestic tasks and women underestimate, making accurate information difficult to obtain. j

However, feminist sociologists have made us look at the roles played by men and women inside the family. Some have linked these roles to patriarchy and capitalism. While there are some changes, it seems that women still carry the greatest burden of housework and childcare, even when they go out to work. k

e 16/20 marks awarded. A good introduction, referring to Item A but not simply copying from it. a The reference is expanded by identifying the view as a functionalist one, and showing knowledge of the correct terms for the male and female roles. b The next part also uses material from the Item about Oakley, but develops this, referring to the method used and some of the findings. c Some evaluation is then shown by the mention that Oakley's research was carried out some time ago and also refers to an important change since that time.

d The next part again uses material from the Item. e But it uses it to claim that findings do not support the expressed view. f There are then some relevant examples. g and h These are followed by further evaluation asking whether more recent evidence has shown a change. i A counter-view to the feminists is given.

j A good point is made by raising the problems of obtaining accurate information on this topic. **k** The conclusion seems rather rushed and doesn't really summarise and evaluate the feminist contribution. The student probably spent too much time on the previous question and had to finish in a hurry – a reminder of the importance of good time management. It is a shame that no reference was made in the answer to class and ethnic differences. However, there is evidence of all three skills and this is a competent answer.

Overall mark: 36/40

> **Student B**
>
> **1**   Domestic division of labour means that the woman does most of the housework and childcare while the man does gardening and DIY.

e **1/2 marks awarded.** The student gives an example of the domestic division of labour, but doesn't define the term so has not given a complete answer.

> **2**   Increased life expectancy will mean that as women tend to live longer than men, there will be more widows living in single-person households. Also more people will end up in a communal residence like a care home rather than having their own home.

e **2/2 marks awarded.** The first point, about widows in single-person households, would apply even without increased life expectancy, as females on average have always had longer life expectancy than men, but the second point about more communal households is valid and gains the marks. It is sometimes helpful to give a second example if you are not sure.

> **3**   Children have to rely on their parents for longer, so have lower status than when children had to go out to work at a young age and help with the family finances.
>
> Children have become an important consumer market, with clothes, toys, games and films designed especially for them, which gives them more status than when they were just 'seen but not heard'.
>
> Children have to stay in education longer.

e **4/6 marks awarded.** The first two points are fine, though it would have been better in the first to say why children have to rely on their parents for longer – this is implied in the second part, but not made explicit. The third point is not related to status and is close to echoing the first point about dependency, so gains no marks.

4   Fathers in Victorian times were meant to be very strict and didn't have much to do with their children, as this was seen as the mother's role, or the nanny if it was a rich family. a

Although in the Second World War lots of women went out to work in factories and driving buses, etc., after the war when the men came home women were once again 'the housewife' and the man's main role was the breadwinner. Looking after children was seen as 'women's work' and the role of the father was to provide a home and put food on the table. b

In the 1960s, though, Goldthorpe and Lockwood in their 'Affluent worker' study of working-class car workers found that these workers were becoming more home and family-centred. c

Things began to change in the 1980s with the appearance of the so-called 'new man'. The new man was someone who wasn't afraid to change a nappy or push his baby around in a buggy, as well as helping his wife with the housework and shopping. The role of father was seen as being more caring and sensitive. d

Although the term 'new man' seems to have disappeared, the role of father is still mainly like this. With most women going out to work, and more men being made redundant, especially from traditional working-class manual jobs, lots of men have had to take over, or share, many jobs once seen as 'women's work', including looking after children. We even have 'stay-at-home dads' who take on the housework and childcare job full-time while their wife or partner is the breadwinner. e

We have to remember that there are nearly 2 million lone-parent families in Britain and 8% of these are men, so many children don't have a father living with them, and around 160,000 men are bringing up a child or children on their own. f

The views of society about the role of fathers have definitely changed over the last 70 years. Fathers nowadays are expected to be far more involved with their children than they used to be – seeing them born, taking paternity leave to bond with a new baby, playing with their toddlers, going to parents' evenings to talk about the children's progress, etc. In many ways, the roles of mothers and fathers have become very similar, though this is not true in all families. g

e **5/10 marks awarded.** This is an example of an answer in which the examiner has to work very hard to find where the relevant points are. The best way of answering this type of question is always to keep your two sections (in this case the 'two ways') quite separate.

a The first sentence is irrelevant as it is well outside the timescale of 70 years. b The next part is acceptable as an introduction as it describes how the role of father was seen at roughly the start of the 70-year period, allowing the changes to be demonstrated.

c The reference to Goldthorpe and Lockwood, which could have been made relevant, is just stated and not linked to the question at all. d Finally, the question begins to be addressed, with reference to the 'new man' and fathers. e This is further developed by bringing it more up to date and showing analysis in why some men have had to change their role within the family. f The point about lone-parent families again contains potentially relevant material, but this is not made explicit. g The final sentences give further examples of changes in fathers' roles, make the interesting point about increased similarity in the roles of mothers and fathers, and hint at differences in different groups, though this is not explained.

Overall, some good points made, although some not developed, with some analysis, but a poorly constructed answer.

5 Before feminist sociologists appeared, sociology was a 'malestream' subject. There are different types of feminist – e.g. Marxist, radical, liberal, black – but they tend to look at society in a different way from men, and often choose different topics to study. a

One of the things that many feminist sociologists have looked at is gender roles within the family. This means they look at who does what and sometimes link it to a theory, e.g. Marxism. Oakley looked at the housewife role in the 1970s and talked to middle-class and working-class housewives. Before this, things such as housework had not been considered as a suitable topic to study – it was not seen as important. As the Item says, some sociologists argued that these roles were 'natural'. b Oakley didn't only look at who actually did the housework and looking after the children, she used interviews to find out what the women thought about it. Most of the women in her study thought that being a housewife was boring and felt shut off from 'proper' society – they were alienated. c

About the same time that Oakley was doing her research, Willmott and Young said that families would become more symmetrical, with more equality between the sexes. d

Other feminist sociologists such as Delphy and Leonard, Duncombe and Marsden, Ferri and Smith and Man-Yee Kan have also looked at gender roles in the family and their findings are much the same as Oakley's, although not nearly as many women are now stay-at-home housewives. e This goes against the view in the Item that domestic tasks are now shared more equally. Even if men are doing more than they used to, they are still not doing as much as women, even if the women are working the same hours outside the home as the men are. f

Marxist feminists such as Barrett and McIntosh link the housewife role to patriarchy and capitalism, saying that having women in the housewife and mother role raises the next generation of workers and provides unpaid labour looking after adult male workers. Women are also a 'reserve army of labour', being part of the workforce when needed but able to be 'sent back indoors' when they aren't. g

> Functionalists take a different view of gender roles. They see them as 'natural', or biological, while feminists see them as socially constructed. Parsons said that men's and women's roles were complementary and that this was the best way to benefit society, with men being the breadwinners and decision-makers and women the carers and home-makers. Barrett and McIntosh call this 'the ideology of familism', e.g. a set of ideas to convince society that the nuclear family with segregated gender roles is 'best'. **h**
>
> In conclusion, feminist sociologists have shown us an aspect of the family that was ignored before. They have shown that gender roles have been and are socially constructed rather than biological. Some feminists have linked gender roles to wider aspects such as capitalism and patriarchal ideology. **i**

e **15/20 marks awarded.** **a** A brief introduction with a few relevant points about feminist sociologists generally. **b** The next section begins to focus on the question and shows relevant knowledge of Oakley and her work. The reference to the Item is simply repeating the words, with no elaboration or showing how they are related to the question. You must use (apply) the material in the Item, not simply repeat it. **c** There is more relevant information from Oakley's study, showing good knowledge and understanding. **d** The reference to Willmott and Young is potentially relevant, but is just stated and not developed, so adds nothing. It could have been linked to the last sentence in the Item.

e The list of feminist sociologists is potentially relevant, but as a list it adds little. It is better to take just one or two studies and show their relevance to the topic rather than simply offer a list of names. There is a brief reference to an important change – that not as many women are now full-time housewives. **f** There is an attempt to make the material relevant by the reference to the Item. **g** There is some accurate material on a Marxist feminist view, but although potentially relevant, it is not clearly tied into the question.

h There is some evaluation of the feminist view by contrasting it with functionalist ideas, and the use of Barrett and McIntosh as a criticism of these. The functionalist views could have been linked to the view expressed in the Item.

i There is a good conclusion introducing the important concept of 'social construct' and linking feminist views of gender roles to wider aspects of society.

Overall, some good material here, but also missed opportunities to use and make explicit reference to the information in the Item. Demonstration of all three skills, with some limited evaluation.

Overall mark: 27/40

Question 2

1 Define the term 'fertility rate'. (2 marks)

ⓔ There are several 'rates' in discussion of populations – make sure you choose the right one.

2 Using one example, briefly explain how the modern family could be seen as patriarchal. (2 marks)

ⓔ Note that the question is talking about the modern family, not families in the nineteenth century.

3 Outline three reasons for the increase in cohabitation. (6 marks)

ⓔ Remember that you are asked to 'outline' the reasons – write enough to gain the marks, but avoid lengthy discussions. Put each reason on a new line.

4 Outline and explain two ways in which our ideas of 'childhood' have changed. (10 marks)

ⓔ This is almost a 'compare and contrast' type of question, so for each way you should say how it was in the past and how it has changed. As there are 10 marks available, you could say something brief about why the changes have occurred.

5 Read Item B below and answer the question that follows.

> **Item B**
>
> Many functions that were once carried out by the family, such as the welfare of its members, have been taken over by agencies such as the medical profession and social services. However, the family still performs some essential functions, such as socialising children and producing the next generation.

Applying material from Item B and your knowledge, evaluate the view that the state has taken over most of the functions of the family. (20 marks)

ⓔ Remember to identify the material from the Item that you must use – you have been given an example of a family function now taken over by other bodies and examples of functions that are still carried out by the family. Your knowledge should enable you to add to these. Evaluation should be shown by assessing, with examples and evidence, whether and to what extent the view expressed in the question can be upheld. Always remember the danger of talking about 'the family' as though all families were the same.

> **Student A**
>
> **1** The fertility rate is the number of live births per 1,000 women of child-bearing age (15–45) per year in a population.

ⓔ **2/2 marks awarded.** This is concise and correct.

2 'Patriarchy' means 'rule by men', so refers to situations where men have power. The modern family can be seen as patriarchal as even when women work outside the home they still do the lion's share of housework and childcare.

ⓔ **2/2 marks awarded.** Again, a brief but accurate example. There was no need to give an explanation of patriarchy, but if it is kept short, this can be helpful just in case the example is not completely clear.

3 When a couple lived together without being married, this used to be called 'living in sin' and was frowned upon. With the decline in religious belief, it has become more socially acceptable.

More women are now going into higher education and having a career. Many want to focus on this and be sure that they are in a relationship with the right person before committing themselves to marriage, so cohabitation is sometimes seen as a 'trial marriage'.

Getting married with the traditional ceremony, flowers, guests, clothes, meals, honeymoon, etc. is now expensive and many young couples need the money to pay their rent or mortgage rather than spend it on a wedding, so often delay the wedding until their finances improve.

ⓔ **6/6 marks awarded.** Three good reasons, clearly explained.

4 'Childhood' is a social construct. That means that each society has ideas at any one time about what it means to be a child. Although biological age obviously comes into it, the stages towards leaving childhood and becoming an adult can be different in different societies and in the same society at different times.

ⓔ A good introduction – brief, but clearly showing understanding of the social nature of definitions of childhood.

One way in which our ideas of childhood have changed is that we have increased the length of time that we consider somebody a child. When life expectancy was short children had to take on what we would think of as adult roles at a very young age – for example hunting, going out to work, even going into battle. In the upper classes especially, children could be married before they were even in their teens. One of the reasons for our lengthening of childhood has been the increase in the amount of time children have to spend in compulsory education. Ideas have changed, and it is now thought that it is better that children get formal teaching about things rather than being taught by their parents or learning a trade on the job like in an apprenticeship. If you are having to go to school, you obviously can't be out at work earning money, so children are dependent on their parents for far longer than they used to be – at least until the age of 16, and usually even longer than that.

ⓔ A good paragraph. The first sentence states clearly what one of the changes is – this is a help both to the student and to the examiner. The answer goes on to explain and give examples of when 'childhood' was shorter, making an interesting point about class differences, and then in the second part explains, with reasons, why this has changed. There is good evidence of analysis – breaking down the reasons into separate parts.

> A second way is that we now have a much better understanding of how children develop. This is quite recent, and comes through the development of psychology and child psychology. Parents are now taught the importance of things such as play and how to develop children's language skills, with educational toys, special children's books and parenting manuals. Again through psychology and psychiatry we know how important childhood is as a preparation for not just the physical side of adulthood but also the mental and emotional side. Society now sees children as individuals who are being shaped, not just as little adults.

ⓔ A sophisticated paragraph linking child development to other disciplines such as psychology. Again, the first sentence sets out another way in which ideas of childhood have changed, then goes on to explain these well. This answer shows clearly a good way of tackling this type of question. Answers should not be too long (only 10 marks and a limited amount of time are available), so every word should count. It is a good technique to state clearly here in the first sentence what it is you intend to discuss, which is your 'outline', and then go on to give your 'explanations' and analysis. **10/10 marks awarded.**

> **5** According to functionalists, every social institution exists in order to benefit society in some way, so the task for sociologists is to work out what that institution does that helps to maintain a stable and peaceful society. **a**
>
> Early functionalists such as Murdoch looked at families in many different societies to try to find out what their essential functions were. He decided that these were the sexual, reproductive, economic and education functions. In developed Western societies not all these functions were carried out by the nuclear family, so Parsons, in the 1950s, said there were two main functions, the primary socialisation of children and the stabilisation of the adult personality. **b**

ⓔ **a** A good brief introduction showing a clear understanding of the functionalist view, then moving on to focus on the family, with reference to two functionalist sociologists. **b** The two viewpoints are clearly explained, showing an understanding of the work and when it was carried out.

One important function, as mentioned in Item B, is the welfare function. This means that families look after their members in every way, including providing food and shelter and caring for the sick and elderly. **c** The Item states that the welfare function has been taken over by other agencies such as the medical profession, who obviously provide health care, and social services, who do things such as child protection and making sure that elderly people are looked after. **d**

Has the welfare function really been taken away from the family though? Even if they receive professional help, parents are expected to care for their babies and children themselves, with the state stepping in either to provide advice and monitoring (e.g. baby clinics) or when things go wrong, such as when child abuse is suspected and a child is taken into care. Also, we know that many grandparents act as essential babysitters and provide childcare, and with student debt and high youth unemployment many parents are still supporting late teenage and even adult children. These seem to be 'essential functions' as many people would struggle if the family didn't provide them. **e**

The Item also says that essential services such as socialising children and producing the next generation are still essential functions performed by the family. **f** The socialisation of children is no longer left entirely to the family, as important secondary socialisation takes place outside the family, such as at school and through the media. The basic socialisation into the norms and values of society is still largely carried out by the family, and obviously it is families who provide the next generation, so in this sense the view is correct. **g**

e **b and c** An early reference is made to the Item and the welfare function is explained. Good knowledge of appropriate concepts is important, though it is not always essential to explain. Here, though, it is appropriate. **d** Further reference to the Item is made, but the material is developed a little, rather than just being copied. **e** The next paragraph shows evaluation by questioning whether the welfare function has been taken over by the state and providing evidence of welfare still provided by families. **f and g** The next paragraph goes back to the Item and analyses the two functions mentioned to see whether these are still carried out by the family.

It is true that in today's society, many functions that used to be carried out by the family are now at least partly carried out by other state agencies. Is it true, though, to say that 'most' of the functions have been taken over? The evidence seems to suggest that some functions such as education have been largely taken over, though most families still play a part in the education of their children, while many aspects of others, such as welfare, are still carried out by family members, especially women. **h**

It is also true that some families get more state intervention than others. Families with members with long-standing illnesses obviously get more medical help than ones where people are healthy. Some families like the 'troubled families' David Cameron talks about get a lot more intervention from social services and other agencies than other families. ▯

In conclusion, I would say that while the state plays a much greater role in family life than it did in the past, it is not universally true that the state has taken over 'most' of the functions of the family. ▯

ⓔ The last three paragraphs show good evaluation. ▯ The first questions the word 'most', giving evidence of the continuing importance of families. ▯ The second draws attention to the fact that some families receive more state intervention than others, showing good contemporary knowledge of a particular social policy. ▯ Finally, the student offers a firm conclusion in the light of the evidence presented. Note that it is not always possible to come to such a conclusion – there will be occasions where the evidence is inconclusive, or dependent on who is making the judgement, so don't be afraid to say if this is the case.

Overall, this is a sophisticated answer and one that few students would be able to achieve. It shows good analysis and evaluation, and the material in the Item is applied in a relevant way. It provides some useful guidelines as to how exam questions might be tackled and is something to work towards. **20/20 marks awarded.**

Overall mark: 40/40

Student B

1   The fertility rate is the total number of babies born to women of child-bearing age in a given year. The fertility rate has been falling but has recently gone up a little due to younger migrants coming in.

ⓔ **1/2 marks awarded.** The definition is incorrect – it is a 'rate', so will always be 'out of' something, in this case the number of babies per 1,000 women of child-bearing age. However, there is some understanding of the concept, though the second sentence was unnecessary.

2   Despite women's gains, men still have most of the power.

ⓔ **0/2 marks awarded.** There is simply not enough accurate material here. There is some hint of an understanding of patriarchy with the reference to power, but the example is insufficient.

3   With the rises in the divorce rate, many couples want to make sure they are suited before getting married, so live together first. Divorces can be messy and expensive so many couples want to avoid them. As more and more people cohabit it becomes seen as something normal, so there is not as much stigma and social disapproval as there used to be. Parents aren't shocked any more if their children live together without getting married – in fact, many parents themselves cohabit with a second relationship. People don't see the point of getting married.

🅔 **4/6 marks awarded.** The first two points (wanting to avoid a divorce and the decline of social stigma) are accurate and score, but the last one is not explained or developed, so doesn't gain marks. It is much better to separate out your points to make each one clearly visible.

4   Some people believe that childhood is the age of innocence. We have all kinds of rules to protect children, such as CRB checks on adults and age ratings on films and games. 🅐 In past times, children were exposed to all kinds of things that would not be allowed today. Children would have regularly seen animals giving birth and being slaughtered, especially if they lived in the countryside. Also, as death rates were so high, especially infant mortality rates, most children would have experienced a death in the family at a young age, and would probably have seen corpses and attended funerals. Children except those from the upper classes 🅑 went out to work as young as age ten, and would have been exposed to dangerous substances in factories. Young children were at work in the cotton mills where there was dangerous machinery, and they were even sent down the coal mines. Some children in the mines started work at two in the morning and worked an 18-hour day, often doing heavy work like pushing loaded coal trucks through the galleries. This kind of thing would never be acceptable today – children are seen as being in need of protection from harm, both mentally and physically.

🅔 🅐 The first sentence talks about the age of innocence and some of the ways in which children are now protected, but the rest of the material is not really focused on this. However, there are some valid and relevant points giving examples of the kinds of things to which children 'in past times' (no periods specified) were exposed. 🅑 A good, though undeveloped, point is made about class differences in the experience of childhood. The last sentence returns to a focus on the question of 'change'.

In contrast to this view, some argue that childhood has now become 'toxic'. 🅐 Even though children have to stay at school at least until the age of 16, and in that sense are treated as children, there are many other things in society that take away the idea of childhood innocence. 🅑 Children used to be dressed in clothes thought appropriate for children, but now many, especially girls, are encouraged to wear clothes that emphasise sexuality, even from quite a young age. Girls didn't use to wear make-up until their late teens, or at least until they left school, but now make-up is aimed at very young girls. Even though there is a watershed for TV programmes, so 'adult' things aren't shown until later in the evening, most children now have access to the internet and social media and can watch things their parents might not approve of. Even the news in the early bulletins will be talking about things such as rape and child abuse, and there are explicit photos of nude or barely dressed women on show in magazines and newspapers. Some people started a campaign to stop *The Sun* 'Page Three' photos. The emphasis on being slim has led to even very young girls being so worried about their figure that they have become anorexic. So although society might pay lip service to children being seen as innocent and in need of protection, as they were in the 1950s for example, we allow many things that go against this idea and expose children to a lot of adult material and pressures. **c**

e **a** A good beginning that shows what this section is going to be about. **b** The answer sets up the contrast between one way in which dependency creates 'children' with those things that seem to contradict this. There is then a range of relevant examples to show how childhood can be seen as 'toxic'. **c** The final sentence is an appropriate conclusion to what has gone before. The answer is largely descriptive and heavily dependent on examples, of which there are probably too many, but there is some attempt at analysis and the examples are relevant to the point being made. **8/10 marks awarded.**

5 Functionalists believe that societies are stable and harmonious. They say that society is like a human body, where all the different parts such as limbs and organs like the heart and kidneys have a particular function to play, and when they all work together each one doing what it is supposed to do, then the body is healthy. Sometimes though things go wrong and a body part becomes diseased, so it is then dysfunctional. **a**

Functionalists see the family as being one of the 'body parts' of society, with a role to play to make sure that society stays healthy. Murdoch, an early functionalist, looked at families in different parts of the world and decided that the basic nuclear family was universal, which proved what an important part it had to play. **b**

Before the welfare state and other important social changes, families had to do everything for their members. Before industrialisation families worked together in or around the home to produce goods and food. There was no universal medical service and only rich people could afford doctors, so families looked after members when they were ill, and when people started working in factories, you usually got your job through someone in your family 'speaking' for you. **c** Nowadays, as Item B says, many functions that were once carried out by the family, such as the welfare of its members, have been taken over by agencies such as the medical professions and social services. **d**

Parsons, another functionalist, said that the family still performed two essential functions, which were the socialisation of children and the stabilisation of the adult personality. **e** Functionalists believe that gender roles played by men and women should be different as women are by nature more caring and men are more logical and able to make decisions. **f**

Families do still socialise children, by teaching them to speak their native language and showing them what the norms and values of their society are. Children are not only socialised by the family, though – they come into contact with peer groups, teachers and the output of the mass media, which might teach them different things. **g**

The Item says that the state has taken over most of the functions of the family. However, families are still important. ▇ You don't call a doctor because a child has a fall and cuts their knee, one of the parents (usually the mother) will deal with it. This is part of the welfare function. Although there are benefits like unemployment benefit and old age pensions, many families will give financial or other help to unemployed grown-up children, like letting them live at home, and will provide unpaid care for aged relatives. ▇

So while the state does some things that families used to do, I would not agree that the state has taken over most of the functions of the family. ▇

ⓔ 12/20 marks awarded. ▇ The introduction is too long and does not focus on the question. While it is acceptable to show that you recognise the basic functionalist viewpoint, it is important to make your answer relevant to the question asked. ▇ There is then a mention of the family, but again this drifts off the point. ▇ The third paragraph begins to home in on the question by showing some of the functions that used to be carried out by the family. ▇ This is followed by a mention of the Item, but the words are simply copied out and there is no comment or development. You must show that you are applying (using) the material in the Item.

▇ There is a potentially relevant reference to Parsons, but this is not integrated into the answer – it is just a 'gobbet' of knowledge. ▇ The reference to gender roles, while accurate, is not tied into the question. ▇ The next paragraph implicitly refers to Parsons by talking of the socialisation function, and then shows that families are not alone in performing the socialisation function, though this is not linked to the role of the state. **h and i** The penultimate paragraph refers again to the Item, but this time engages with it by pointing out that families are still important – though the word 'functions' could have usefully been used here – and providing relevant examples. ▇ The conclusion, although stating an opinion, adds little to the debate. The knowledge presented is largely accurate, but of limited depth and not always focused on the question. The Item is not used as fully as it should be, and evaluation is weak and undeveloped and consists mainly of simply presenting evidence that appears to contradict the view expressed in the question. However, there is some understanding of the functionalist view of the role of the family, together with knowledge of some functions of the family in the past and present.

Overall mark: 25/40

Question 3

1 Define the term 'industrialisation'. (2 marks)

ⓔ Don't confuse this with 'urbanisation', although the two are linked.

2 Using one example, briefly explain how migration may affect the structure of a population. (2 marks)

ⓔ The focus is on the 'structure', not the size, of the population.

3 Outline three reasons for possible changes in power relationships within the family. (6 marks)

ⓔ The question talks about 'possible' changes, so you don't have to challenge this or think about changes that would affect every family.

4 Outline and explain two ways in which the growth of urbanisation affected household structures. (10 marks)

ⓔ Make sure that both your ways focus on 'urbanisation', and also household structures rather than roles.

5 Read Item C below and answer the question that follows.

> ### Item C
> Changes in patterns of marriage have caused concern in many parts of society. The growth in both cohabitation and lone-parent families and the increase in the number of 'singletons' are used as evidence that marriage is no longer viewed as important.

Applying material from Item C and your knowledge, evaluate the view that marriage is no longer an important institution in society. (20 marks)

ⓔ You must refer to the evidence cited in the Item as part of your answer. Evaluation could be shown by arguing why these factors, and others that you might include, do not necessarily support the view stated in the question. You should also think of evidence that could be used to support the view that marriage is still important.

> ### Student A
> **1** Industrialisation is the process where a society moves from being a mainly agricultural one to one based on the manufacture of goods, typically in factories using machines.

ⓔ **2/2 marks awarded.** A clear and accurate definition.

2 If we are talking about inward migration (immigration) and if the immigrants are mainly in the younger age groups, this will alter the overall structure of the population by increasing the proportion of people in those age groups in the population as a whole, which will help to balance out an ageing population.

As many of these younger immigrants are likely to be women of child-bearing age they are also likely to increase the overall birth rate.

ⓔ **2/2 marks awarded.** Two examples are given here and both are correct, though only one will gain the marks.

3 *Reason one*: women have more power with regard to financial decisions as many wives are now in employment, therefore are bringing money into the household, whereas before it used to be mainly the husbands who did this. As wage earners, they will feel they have more say.

Reason two: many women are cohabiting with their partner, rather than being married to him, so they are completely independent as far as the law is concerned. They will usually have their own bank account.

Reason three: another way that power relationships have changed is that children now have more legal rights. They can consent to their own dental or medical treatment from the age of 16, girls can be put on the pill without their parents' consent, and all children have the right at any age to be heard in a court of law. Unfortunately, as recent cases of child sex abuse have shown, children are still often not believed when they report ill-treatment.

ⓔ **5/6 marks awarded.** Three acceptable reasons given. Reasons one and three are well explained, but the explanation offered for reason two is not clearly linked to power relationships, so only 1 mark for this.

4 Urbanisation is the movement of people away from the countryside to living in towns. As industrialisation developed in the eighteenth and nineteenth centuries, there was a huge movement of people away from small towns and villages to live in the large urban centres that grew up round the mills, mines and factories.

ⓔ A good, brief introduction that shows a clear understanding of the concept of urbanisation. It is not essential, however, to provide an introduction in this type of question.

It was suggested by functionalists such as Talcott Parsons that there is a 'fit' between the type of economy in a society and the dominant type of family structure. The belief was that pre-industrial societies were characterised by extended 'multi-functional' households and industrial ones by nuclear households. ａ However, work by Laslett showed that in pre-industrial England there was already a high proportion of nuclear households, and Anderson showed that in Preston at the height of industrialisation extended households were common, as people arriving from the countryside to the new towns depended on kin to help them find work and often lived with relatives in extended family households. **b** So early urbanisation did affect household structures, but not in the way that some people suggested. It seems that at least in the early stages of urbanisation there was a growth in the proportion of extended household structures. **c**

e It is good practice in this type of question to 'outline' each reason and then provide a suitable explanation. **a** The first two sentences outline a possible relationship between urbanisation and household structures. **b** The next part explains how research showed that the effect of industrialisation was different from that expected. **c** The final two sentences conclude the explanation, linking it back to the question.

Another way in which urbanisation affected household structures was found by Willmott and Young in their study of working-class families in Bethnal Green, in East London. They found a community characterised by groups of families living not together in extended families under the same roof, but living close by each other and with a great deal of daily face-to-face contact. They termed this type of family structure 'local extended families', because although not living together, they behaved almost as though they did. **d** These families were also called 'matrifocal', because at the heart of each larger group was 'Mum', usually the wife's mother, who seemed to hold the family together. **e** This shows how later urbanisation in one way broke up the traditional extended family, mainly because houses were too small for several families, but created another type. **f**

e **d** This section outlines a relationship between urbanisation and household structure by referring to a relevant piece of research and giving a brief summary of relevant findings. **e** The next sentence, though accurate, could have been omitted as it is not strictly related to household structure. **f** The final sentence sums up neatly and refers back to the question.

More recently, the growth of urbanisation and other factors in society **g** has led to even more different types of household, with an increase in the number of people living alone or sharing with non-related people and not being in a relationship with them, and also lone-parent families. There is also now a process of de-urbanisation, as changes in working practices and technology mean that people can move away from towns back to the countryside and work from home. **h**

e Given the time constraints of an exam, and given that this question is worth 10 marks, this section could have been left out. **g** The student shows awareness that 'other factors in society' are now being discussed, which has moved away from the question asked. **h** The final section is also not relevant. While you will not be penalised for giving additional information not related to the question, it is not advisable as it is using up valuable time and will not gain you extra marks. However, there is sufficient relevant material here to gain full marks. **10/10 marks awarded.**

> **5**   Many people, including some politicians and those holding New Right views of the family, believe that marriage has been undermined and is no longer seen as important. **a** As Item C says, cohabitation and lone-parent families have both increased. More people live together without being married and there are now nearly 2 million lone parents. **b** But does this mean that people don't think marriage is important?

e **a, b** Identification of some who hold the view expressed in the question and reference to the Item. However, apart from mentioning the number of lone parents, the material in the Item has not (at least yet) been applied.

> There are several reasons why people cohabit rather than getting married. These include waiting to see if they get on well enough to live together for a long time (a kind of trial marriage), the cost of a wedding, which can run into thousands of pounds, or the fact that they can't legally marry because one of them (or even both) is still married to somebody else and is waiting for a divorce. None of these things really means that people don't believe that marriage is important. **c**

e Some reasons given for cohabitation. **c** A hint of evaluation, but this is not developed.

> Another reason for cohabitation is that until very recently, same-sex couples could not legally marry. When that is the case, they have no choice but to live together without being married. 'Couples' and 'families' doesn't only mean heterosexual people. **d** If marriage is not seen as important, why did so many people campaign to allow same-sex marriages? Even when civil partnerships were allowed, many gay people still wanted to be allowed to marry, showing that they thought it was an important institution. **e**

e **d** Another reason for cohabitation, with an important point about how 'couples' and 'families' are defined. **e** A good point offering the campaign for same-sex marriage as evidence of the importance of marriage.

As for lone parents, these are often the result of a relationship (not necessarily marriage) breakdown. Research by the Centre for Family Research showed that there was a group of women who were 'single mothers by choice' – that is, they had deliberately chosen to have a child even though they weren't in a relationship. However, the interviews with these women showed that they would have preferred to have been in a heterosexual nuclear family unit, they just hadn't met the 'right man', and so wanted to be mothers that they had gone ahead anyway. Most of them managed because of the help and support they got from their parents and siblings.

e This is interesting, but is not specifically linked to marriage.

Some people from the New Right, such as Charles Murray and politicians such as Iain Duncan Smith, blame increased crime (especially teenage crime) and even people being 'work shy' and wanting to live on benefits on what they see as the breakdown of the family and the decline in marriage. However, not all crime is committed by young people with cohabiting parents or lone parents, and people from all types of family are living on benefits. **f**

e **f** This shows what some people see as effects of the decline in marriage, with an evaluative point showing some evidence to the contrary.

There are good arguments for saying that marriage is still regarded as important. Most cohabiting couples go on to marry, especially if they have children. Nine out of ten people getting married now have cohabited at some point. Many lone parents also form new relationships, so 'lone parent status' is often temporary. Two-thirds of all households consist of married couples, with or without children. **g**

Finally, marriage is still an important institution in law. So-called 'common law spouses' have no legal recognition, and inheritance laws are based on legal marriages. **h** In postmodern times we have to accept that what we think of as 'the family' is changing, and there are many different family forms nowadays, but the evidence still shows that marriage is an important institution in society. **i**

e **g, h, i** Some relevant evidence provided to show how marriage is still important and a brief conclusion that tries to sum up the arguments and evidence presented. While some of the material in the Item was used, there was no reference to the potentially important point about the 'singletons', those apparently not wishing to marry or cohabit. Not all the material presented was clearly focused on the question. Some analysis and evaluation, though not always developed. **16/20 marks awarded.**

Overall mark: 35/40

Student B

1 Where people don't work from home making things by hand but go to factories.

e **1/2 marks awarded.** Some understanding, but not sufficient for both marks.

2 If a lot of people leave a country and if they are in roughly the same age group, this can leave a 'gap' in the population. For example, a lot of young Polish people have left Poland to work abroad where they earn more money, and so there aren't as many young adults in Poland as there would otherwise be.

e **2/2 marks awarded.** An interesting answer in that it focuses on the effects of emigration rather than the usual immigration. A good and accurate example with an appropriate explanation.

3 'Women's lib' has shown women that they do not have to depend on a man – they can be his equal. Women can now apply for a divorce and can live independently, so a woman has the power to leave a marriage if she is not satisfied. It used to be only men who could apply for a divorce.

It is now the norm for women to be wage earners, even if they have a husband/partner, so sharing the costs of the household gives them more power. Women used to be housewives not earning anything and were given 'housekeeping money' by their husbands.

e **4/6 marks awarded.** The first reason is not clearly explained or linked to power relationships, so does not score. The other two each gain full marks.

4 Urbanisation means when most people in a population live in towns and cities rather than in small villages. This started to happen in England in the Industrial Revolution, and now about 80% of the UK population lives in an urban area. **a**

e **a** Two brief sentences which, however, show an understanding of the concept of urbanisation, and knowledge of when it began to develop in England and the proportion of urban dwellers today.

One effect of urbanisation is an increase in geographical mobility, which means that people move away from the area they were born in. This is usually because there is not much work in rural areas except in agriculture so people have to go and live where the work is. This means the break-up of the extended family. **b** People often now live up to hundreds of miles away from their parents, grandparents and siblings, as families become dispersed. They end up in 'isolated nuclear families', cut off from their kin. This has changed, though, as people can now keep in touch with their relatives using the phone, email and social media. **c**

e **b** A good point linking geographical mobility to household structure with some analysis, though reference to Anderson's work would have been helpful. The useful concept of the 'isolated nuclear family' is introduced. **c** It is not made clear how the last sentence is linked to the question.

> Urbanisation also affects the birth rate. Children aren't as much use to families in urban areas as they are in rural ones, and urban birth rates are lower than rural ones. **d**

e This is a potentially important second point. **d** However, it is left completely undeveloped and there is only the briefest explanation of why urban birth rates should be lower than rural ones. **5/10 marks awarded.**

> **5** Most people in society used to get married. People tended not to live together until they were married as 'living in sin' was something shocking and shameful. **a** If a girl got pregnant her family usually made the couple get married as quickly as possible – this was known as a 'shotgun wedding'. In the 1920s a lot of women couldn't get married as so many young men had been killed in the First World War that there was a 'lost generation', and many women had no choice but to end up as spinsters. After that, though, marriage rates went up and getting married was seen as the normal thing.

e **a** A slightly muddled start, though with a relevant point about why cohabitation was seen as shameful. The points about 'shotgun weddings' and the 'lost generation' aren't really relevant, and the last sentence almost repeats the first.

> We are now living in postmodern society where there is a lot more freedom of choice, and things have changed. As Item C says, cohabitation has increased. Most people seem to live together at least at first, though a lot go on to get married, so it's not that they are against marriage as such. People aren't as religious as they used to be, so there is not as much stigma as there used to be if you have a partner instead of a husband or wife. **b** Item C also talks about lone-parent families, but lone-parent families are often formed after divorce, so the lone parent will have been married at some point. Many marriages break up because people don't want to live together if they are unhappy, so you could say that some marriages break down because they don't live up to what people think marriage should be rather than thinking that it isn't important. **c**

e **b** Appropriate references to the Item, with the material about cohabitation and lone parents applied to the question. **c** There is an important evaluative point at the end.

> Item C talks about 'singletons' – never-married people living alone. There has been a growing number of these in all Western societies. Many people choose this lifestyle status, and these tend to be younger, affluent people with well-paid jobs who have a large number of friends and who tend to live in city centres with lots of amenities. For these people, it seems that marriage isn't important. **d**

(e) d Further reference to the material in the Item, well applied to the question.

> On the other hand, there are people whose singleton status isn't really a matter of choice. With youth unemployment, even for graduates, so high, lots of young people are back living with their parents, and they often have student debts so can't afford their own household, whether in a marriage or cohabiting. e

(e) e An important and evaluative point which links to the previous paragraph and indicates the complexity of discussions about marriage and the extent to which people may or may not have real choices.

> I think what it boils down to is that for some people marriage is an important institution for society but for others it isn't. In postmodern societies people can choose the kind of life they want to lead. f

(e) A rather weak conclusion. f The last point about choice seems to contradict the previous paragraph, which was about the lack of choice for some people. Overall, a fair attempt to use and develop the material in the Item, though the point about the changes in marriage causing 'concern' is ignored. Some good knowledge and understanding, with some analysis and evaluation, though the answer lacks real depth. 14/20 marks awarded.

Overall mark: 26/40

■ The A-level examination

The topic of *Families and households* is examined on Paper 2 of the A-level examination, 'Topics in Sociology'. The question appears in Section A of Paper 2, as 4.2.2, and is one of four options. The *whole* exam lasts for 2 hours, carries 80 marks and is worth one-third of the A-level qualification. The *Families and households* question is one half of the exam and carries 40 marks. You should therefore spend about an hour answering the *Families and households* question, leaving about 25–30 minutes for the last question, which carries 20 marks. Try to manage your time so that you have time to read through the whole paper at the end.

Question 1

1   Outline and explain two ways in which changes in the law have affected women's family roles over the past 60 years.   (10 marks)

ⓔ There are so many state policies that could be mentioned here. Make sure you decide on just two and stick to them. State each policy clearly, then show the ways in which they affected women's roles in the family. Leave a space between the two to differentiate them clearly.

2   Read Item A below and answer the question that follows.

> **Item A**
>
> Almost a third of households in the UK, 7 million in total, are now one-person households. However, people living alone do not form a group sharing the same characteristics. For example, there are more women than men in this group, except in the 35–49 age group, and whites are more likely than Asians or British Asians to live alone.

   Applying material from Item A, analyse two reasons for the increase in one-person households.   (10 marks)

ⓔ Make sure you use (apply) the information provided in the Item for each of your two reasons. Show appropriate analysis by 'unpicking' the relevant information.

3   Read Item B below and answer the question that follows.

> **Item B**
>
> Some sociologists claim that many changes in society have benefited women and their roles within the family. For example, they argue that both the increasing number of women in the workforce and the growing acceptance of equality between the sexes have led to the roles of men and women within the family becoming much more similar. Other sociologists argue that family roles continue to reflect the unequal positions of men and women in society.

   Applying material from Item B and your knowledge, evaluate the view that families remain largely patriarchal structures that disadvantage women.   (20 marks)

ⓔ It is a good idea to start by locating the view stated in the question in its sociological and theoretical context. Identify and then use the material provided in the Item to examine the extent to which it supports the view expressed in the first sentence. Remember to bring in other relevant material from your own knowledge. You will need to examine the extent to which the evidence supports or refutes the view expressed in the question.

Student A

1 One way is the changes relating to domestic violence. This is still a hidden crime because many cases go unreported, but some changes in the law are helping to protect women. **a** Although domestic violence itself is still not a specific crime, it is still a crime to physically assault someone. At the end of 2014 the Home Secretary, Theresa May, announced that 'coercive control', which would include psychological and emotional abuse, would be covered by the Serious Crime Bill, and people convicted could face up to 14 years in prison. **b** This recognises that violence is not always physical in nature. **c** Other legal changes are that now men can be issued with Domestic Violence Protection Orders, which can prevent them from going near their victim for up to 28 days. This can give the woman time to make arrangements, such as going to a refuge or other place of safety, or find out what her options are. **d** From 2014 there is also what is known as Clare's Law, or Domestic Violence Disclosure, which gives women the right to ask police if their actual or prospective partner has a history of domestic violence. This may help to prevent women getting into situations where domestic violence is likely. **e** These changes are unlikely to stop domestic violence, but give women more legal protection from domestic violence than they had in the past. **f**

e **a** An accurate and detailed discussion of some legal changes relating to domestic violence. The useful concept of 'hidden crime' is introduced. **b and c** A specific change is mentioned with some analysis of why it is important. **d and e** Another change is given and explained, and a further one. **f** The final point again shows some analysis and clearly relates the answer back to the question.

Other legal changes which have benefited women are those relating to legal abortion. **g** The Abortion Act of 1967 made abortion legal under certain conditions. This was particularly important for working-class women trying to escape from the burden of large families. **h** While wealthier women could often pay a psychiatrist to say that they needed an abortion to avoid extreme psychological distress, poorer women either had the child or resorted to so-called 'back-street abortionists', often with dreadful consequences. Around 40 women a year died from botched abortions or subsequent infections. **i** There have been changes to the abortion laws, and some people are still trying to get the legal limit lowered, but allowing abortions to take place under proper medical conditions has helped many women, both married and unmarried. Before the changes in the law, some young women were faced with having to give up their baby for adoption at birth in order for them to continue with their studies or to avoid the stigma of being an unmarried mother. **j** It is important to remember that not all British women have this legal right. Abortion is still illegal in Northern Ireland. **k**

e **g** Another relevant area of change is identified. **h and i** The important point about class differences is made and further explained. **j and k** There is relevant discussion of how the legal changes have helped some women, with an important concluding evaluative point regarding differences within the UK. Overall, an accurate and detailed discussion that answers the question and demonstrates good skill levels. **10/10 marks awarded.**

2   As Item A states, one-person households now form a large proportion of all households, and the number is showing steady growth. However, as the Item also states, we cannot talk of 'one-person households' as though they are all the same – there are many different reasons for people living alone. For some it is a choice, for others it is a necessity brought on by circumstances. **a**

One reason for the increase is family breakdown. **b** Many couples, whether married or cohabitees, now split up. If there are children involved, the most common scenario is that the children live with the mother, forming a lone-parent or a reconstituted family, if the mother has a new partner, possibly with children of his own, but the father moves out of the family home and sets up a one-person household. If there are no children in the relationship, and if neither partner goes on to live with someone else, then two single-person households are formed. However, many of these will be only temporary, as people often find another partner and live with them. The fact that a common scenario is for the divorced or separated father to live alone explains why men outnumber women in the 35–49 age group, as stated in the Item (the average age for a man to divorce is 45). **c**

It is also pointed out that more whites than Asians or British Asians live alone, and this is explained by the fact that extended families are more common in the Asian community than the white. Even if they do not live under the same roof, such families are often very close-knit, and while marriage breakdown is less common among Asians than the white community, if this happens, one or both partners would probably end up living with a relative rather than living alone. **d**

e **a** A good introduction referring briefly to the Item but adding to it. **b** The second paragraph clearly states a reason and then goes on to show good knowledge and understanding of the groups involved. **c** Good use is made of the Item, showing analysis. **d** Further reference and good analysis is shown in a further use of the Item.

Another reason is the growth of people who choose to live alone – the so-called 'singletons'. **e** Many of these are relatively affluent and live in urban areas. Some are so-called 'metrosexuals', a hybrid of metropolitan homosexuals, but others are 'straight' but prefer to live alone. For many of these people, a circle of close-knit friends has taken the place of family, and they are not lonely. **f** Some have linked the rise of the young, affluent single person to the postmodern idea of the 'cult of the individual'. Such people often have a high investment in 'the self', spending money on clothes, grooming products and social activities. **g** Research has shown that people who never marry are no less content than those that do, and many say they are happier than those who are divorced or were in a failed relationship.

e [e] Another appropriate reason is clearly stated. [f] Good knowledge is shown of the group. [g] Analysis is shown by offering a possible reason for the rise of this type of household.

Two appropriate reasons are given, good knowledge and understanding of each is shown, the material in the Item is used (applied) appropriately and there is good analysis of each. **10/10 marks awarded.**

---

3 The statement that families remain largely patriarchal structures that disadvantage women comes from a feminist viewpoint. [a] While there are different kinds of feminism – radical, liberal, Marxist, etc. – all feminists focus on the position of women in the society. Many feminists believe that the inequality of gender roles in the family is, as the question suggests, the result of patriarchy, but Marxist feminists believe that gender inequality stems from the built-in inequalities of capitalism. [b]

---

e [a] A good beginning that identifies the statement as coming from a feminist perspective. [b] Some brief but accurate and relevant knowledge of different types of feminism.

As far as the family is concerned, feminists have looked particularly at women's roles. Oakley's early study of women and housework showed that most of the women she interviewed did almost all of the housework and childcare (middle-class women were slightly better off in this respect) and found their domestic tasks unrewarding and alienating. [c] Feminist Delphy argues that the housewife role was actually created by patriarchy, as it benefits men so much. [d]

---

e [c] An appropriate reference to Oakley in the context of feminist research, with knowledge of relevant findings. [d] A useful reference to Delphy.

However, Oakley's research was done in the 1970s, when most women, particularly mothers, were 'stay-at-home' housewives and the idea of the 'new man' had not yet surfaced. [e] The Item suggests that things have changed for the better as far as women are concerned. It is true that it is now considered quite normal for mothers, even those with young children, to be in the employed workforce, even though some work only part-time when the children are very small. Some women are now the main breadwinner in their family, as many 'male' jobs have declined or disappeared and the kinds of service work associated with women have seen an increase. [f] But has this been of benefit to women in the family?

---

e [e and f] Some evaluative comments about the time of Oakley's research, followed by appropriate reference to the Item and some brief analysis.

More recent research suggests not. Man-Yee Kan found that women still did more domestic and childcare work than men, though she found that highly educated middle-class women were less unequal than working-class women, which she put down to their higher income giving them more bargaining power in the relationship. Evidence from British Social Attitudes surveys continues to find women doing more household work than their partners, even when both go out to work. Hochschild refers to this as women's 'second shift' – they do the working shift then come home and do the domestic one. g

e g An answer to the question posed at the end of the last paragraph, and appropriate knowledge of some other research on this topic.

The Item suggests that ideas of growing equality between the sexes have led to men's and women's domestic roles becoming more similar. This sounds like the ideas of Willmott and Young on the 'symmetrical family'. h In fact, many would argue with the idea that there is growing equality between the sexes. Even with laws such as the Sex Discrimination Act and the Equal Pay Act, women still earn less on average than men, and are often subject to sexual harassment in the workplace. Many occupations have a 'glass ceiling' keeping women in the lower positions. i

e Reference to other material in the Item. h It would have been appropriate to say a little more about the idea of the 'symmetrical family'. i Analysis and evaluation of the idea of growing equality between the sexes, though moving slightly away from the focus on the family.

This ties in with the idea of patriarchy, which means 'rule by men'. j While women have more power and legal rights than they used to, there is still plenty of evidence that men hold most of the power in society. Although on average men do more housework and childcare than they used to, it is still less than their female partners. 'Looking after the children' is still seen as mainly a woman's responsibility, shown by the fact that in divorce settlements, custody is usually given to the woman. k

e j and k Knowledge shown of what is meant by 'patriarchy', with an example to show society's attitudes towards women's responsibilities, though this is not really linked to the earlier discussion of power.

Some women are also subject to the abuse of power in family relationships. It has been estimated that one in four women will experience some form of domestic violence in her lifetime, and it is still difficult for women to get the help and support they need in these cases. Partly it is because it is often a 'hidden crime', and partly because women are often not believed when they do report abuse. The fact that many women's refuges are closing through lack of funding shows that this is still an issue that is not taken seriously enough. l

e ⟦The issue of power is picked up here, looking at it from the angle of abuse of power, and somewhat implicitly linked to the issue of patriarchy.

> In conclusion, we can probably say that the roles of men and women in the family have, at least for some, become less unequal, but the evidence shows that both society and families are still largely patriarchal structures that disadvantage women. **m**

e A fairly bland conclusion, though related to the previous discussion, and showing awareness of differences between groups. **m** An attempt to provide an answer to the question. **16/20 marks awarded.**

Overall, some good, relevant material, some of which could have been developed a little further. Appropriate use of the material in the Item and some evidence of both analysis and evaluation.

Overall mark: 36/40

> **Student B**
>
> **1** Women have definitely been helped by changes to the divorce laws. **a** In the nineteenth century only men could get a divorce and many women were trapped in unhappy, loveless and sometimes violent marriages. **b** The Divorce Law Reform Act of 1969 ended the idea of 'fault' and said that the only grounds for divorce were 'the irretrievable breakdown of marriage'. Before this, one partner had to be found guilty of a particular offence, usually adultery. **c** A result of this change in the law was that the divorce rate shot up, with more women than men asking for a divorce. It seems likely that lots of people, especially women, were unhappy in their marriage but could not legally divorce. **d**

e **a** An area of legal changes has been correctly identified. **b** The section about the nineteenth century is irrelevant as it falls outside the time frame given in the question – always note carefully if a particular date is mentioned. **c and d** The change in the law is accurately described and mention is made of one of the consequences, with some brief analysis.

> A second change that has helped women is the introduction of civil partnerships in 2005 and same-sex marriage in 2014. **e** While these changes benefit men as well as women, they give gay women the right to enter into a partnership or marriage with their female partner. **f** While some gay women did live with their partner in the past, it tended to be in secrecy and not many women would have done it. They would have been subject to stigma and abuse, and they also had no legal rights as a couple. **g** These changes have helped to establish same-sex families as a valid type of family, not just as a couple, but increasingly as a gay couple with children. **h**

e **e and f** Another relevant area is identified with the point made about benefits to men as well as women. **g** There is some brief analysis about the situation previously. **h** There is a final evaluative point linking the legal changes to different types of family. Overall, a competent though brief answer that sticks to the question (apart from the time slip) and shows some evidence of skills. **5/10 marks awarded.**

> **2** As the Item shows, there are now a lot of one-person households. One reason is that we are now all living longer, and the average life expectancy of women is greater than men, so there are a lot of older people, especially women, living alone. **a** In the past, when people didn't move about so much, older people would be able to move in with one of their children, but extended families are now dispersed and people often live a long way from their parent(s). **b** The task of looking after older parents would usually fall to the woman, but now most women go out to work, so even if they live nearby, it is not possible for them to take in and look after elderly relatives. Many houses are quite small and there would not be room to take an extra person in anyway. **c**

e **a** An appropriate reason is given with reference to life expectancy. **b and c** Some analysis and evaluation of this reason. No specific reference to the material provided in the Item, though clearly the issue of gender has been picked up. Nothing about the difference in a particular age group, though this is potentially helpful information.

> Asian and British Asian culture puts more emphasis on family responsibility than whites do, so it would be less common for an older person to live alone. **d** Also, many of these families are larger than the average white family, so there are more children to share the task. Many Asians live in close-knit communities so their families aren't as dispersed as white families. **e**

e Again, while the discussion of differences between ethnic groups is based on material in the Item, this is not spelled out. **d and e** A suggested reason is given for the difference, with another two provided with very limited analysis. Another reason that could have been suggested is that the age profile of the Asian/British Asian community tends to be younger than that of the white population, so there are fewer older Asians in the population at present. **6/10 marks awarded.**

> **3** Feminists believe that we live in a patriarchal society, where men hold most of the power. **a** This is true in most areas of life, including the family. Feminist and other researchers have shown that looking after the home and children is still thought of as being the main responsibility of the woman and indeed women spend longer on these tasks than men do. Functionalists would say that these roles are 'natural' to women, but feminists argue that our ideas of gender are socially constructed, that is, our values not our biology decide what is 'masculine' and 'feminine'. **b**

ⓔ **ⓐ** A good start that links the notion of patriarchy to the feminist viewpoint. **ⓑ** A contrasting, functionalist, view of women's roles is offered, and the potentially interesting and important point about the social construction of gender is made, though sadly not developed.

> The Item points out that some say that changes in society have benefited women and their family roles. One example given is the growing number of women in the workforce. **ⓒ** It would seem logical to expect that if both partners are working then the household and childcare tasks should be shared equally, but research shows that women still spend more time on these than men, even if they are both out at work. **ⓓ** Some changes that have benefited women are things such as washing machines, dishwashers and ready meals, which mean that women don't have to spend as much time on housework and cooking as their mothers and grandmothers did, but although the overall time might have gone down, women still do more. One argument is that in fact some of these inventions increase the time spent, as people now have higher standards of cleanliness. **ⓔ**

ⓔ **ⓒ** Reference is made to material in the Item. **ⓓ** This is developed, though it would have been better to have referred to at least one piece of research. **ⓔ** The last section risks going off the point – all information included should be relevant to the question.

> Women's roles in the family aren't just about housework and childcare, though. Duncombe and Marsden point out that women's caring role means they are expected to do the 'emotion work' for the family, while Fran Ansley says that women are the 'shit takers'. **ⓕ**

ⓔ **ⓕ** Again, potentially very important points about women's roles, but not explained or developed.

> The Item talks about the equality between the sexes, but feminists would argue against this. There are many ways that women are disadvantaged because of their gender. For example, even though girls now out-perform boys at school, women's average pay is still a lot less than men's, and women find it more difficult to get promotion at work, especially to higher positions. Research has shown that the police, for example, remain highly sexist in their attitudes, both in terms of how they treat women officers and also in their response to things like domestic violence and rape. **ⓖ**

ⓔ **ⓖ** Reference is made to a second piece of material from the Item, but the discussion about lack of equality drifts away from the topic of the family.

> Willmott and Young talked about the symmetrical family and thought there would be greater equality in the home, but this has not happened. **ⓗ** Liberal feminists argue that progress has been made, but radical feminists still see patriarchy as getting in the way of any real equality. Marxist feminists claim that not only are women disadvantaged by patriarchy but also by capitalism, so they have a double disadvantage. **ⓘ**

ⓔ ⒽIt would have been useful to say why Willmott and Young thought there would be greater equality. ⒾAgain, potentially important material about differences between feminists, but not explained or developed. There is no attempt at a conclusion or summing up. **15/20 marks awarded.**

Overall mark: 26/40

Question 2

1   **Outline and explain two ways in which household structures have changed over the past 100 years.**   (10 marks)

ⓔ You have been given quite a long timeline here, so indicate which period(s) you are talking about. A good technique is to treat each of the two ways quite separately, giving the outline and then the explanation for the first, then dealing with the second in a separate paragraph.

2   **Read Item A below and answer the question that follows.**

Item A
Marriage as an institution in the UK remains strong, though there have been many changes. Most marriages are now civil ceremonies, and many are a remarriage for at least one of the partners. The average age of those getting married has also risen.

Applying material from Item A, analyse two changes in patterns of marriage over the past 70 years.   (10 marks)

ⓔ Identify the material in the Item that you need to use, perhaps by underlining it. Remember that you need only address two changes, though you may find that one of your changes could make use of more than one piece of information. Remember to 'analyse' – break down – each change, perhaps by suggesting reasons for it and/or providing additional information.

3   **Read Item B below and answer the question that follows.**

Item B
Some sociologists claim that the small, home-centred nuclear family is ideal for socialising children into the norms and values of society and provides a stable background for both children and their parents. Some politicians go further and argue that the increasing breakdown of such family units is at least partly responsible for such social ills as delinquency and other forms of anti-social behaviour, together with rising rates of depression.

Applying material from Item B and your own knowledge, evaluate the view that the traditional nuclear family best serves the interests of its members and of society as a whole.   (20 marks)

Questions & Answers

(e) Identify the view expressed in the first sentence. Underline all the relevant material provided in the Item to make sure that you use (apply) it to answer the question. Look at the evidence provided for the views expressed in the Item, then show any arguments and evidence against this view to help you come to a conclusion. Remember that you have to show knowledge of this topic beyond that given in the Item.

Student A

1 One way in which household structures has changed over the past 100 years is that households are now likely to contain just nuclear family structures. a According to the 2011 Census, the most common household type was a married or cohabiting couple, with or without children. A century ago many households would have contained a variety of people. Many families had lodgers to help pay the rent money and, as always, the very wealthy would have some live-in servants. Before the welfare state and benefits to help the elderly, many households would contain three generations, as adult children looked after their elderly parents. High death rates left many children as orphans, so often families were looking after their orphaned nieces, nephews or even grandchildren. After the death rates of the First World War there was a shortage of men of marrying age, and many families had a single female 'spinster' relative living with them. Although birth rates fell more or less steadily during the last century, the average family size was bigger than today, so even in families without additional people, the household was likely to be larger as there would have been more children. b

(e) a A good way to start, making clear what the change is. There is no need to repeat the phrasing of the question – it would be acceptable to say 'One way is …'. b The whole of the rest of this section is devoted to analysing and explaining some of the main reasons for this change, showing good knowledge of a range of appropriate reasons.

A second change in household structures is their increasing variety. c Even though the couple type mentioned previously is still predominant, there are now many different types of household. There has been a big rise in one-person households. This has been brought about by longer life expectancy, so a considerable number of older people live alone. There has also been an increase in younger people living alone, particularly in urban areas, and the increase in family breakdown means that many people, especially men, live alone following a divorce or separation. The rise in the number of people going into higher education, together with the high rents associated with many towns and cities, has also meant a growth in households consisting of non-related people, such as groups of students or friends. Recent migrants, especially those who have left families behind in their country of origin, also often live in communal households, usually with others of the same ethnic group, such as Polish or Somalis. The high rates of family breakdown and the lack of stigma associated with being an unmarried mother has also led to an increase in the number of lone-parent households. Changes in the law allowing civil partnerships and single-sex marriages has also increased the number of gay people living together – though when homosexuality stopped being a criminal offence, gay people started living openly together anyway. Finally, there has been a rise in the number of adult children moving back home to live with their parents, which is a result of high unemployment among people coupled with the high rents and costs of housing referred to earlier. **d** Some would argue that this variety in household type is a reflection of postmodern society, where the range of choices to people is greater than ever. **e**

e **c and d** Again, a clear statement of what the identified change is, followed by a range of appropriate explanations with good, accurate detail. **e** An interesting final point linking such changes to postmodern society. **10/10 marks awarded.**

2 One change in patterns of marriage is that it is less popular than it used to be, so a smaller proportion of people are now getting married. **a** The 2011 Census showed that only 47% of people were married, and the media made much of the fact that married people were now in a minority. Of course, many non-married people are living together as though they were married, e.g. cohabiting, something that was once considered shameful. Not only do many people cohabit rather than marry, they also have children outside of marriage, again something that used to carry considerable social stigma. Of those people who do marry, around 70% choose to have a civil rather than a religious ceremony, as stated in the Item, which reflects the declining importance of religion to many people. **b** Again, the vast majority of people who marry have lived together first, which means that the average age of marriage has risen, as the Item states. **c**

e **a** A clear statement of the change that is about to be discussed, followed by a range of possible reasons, showing analysis. **b** Material from the Item is applied rather than just copied. **c** Another relevant reference to the material is made but applied to the question.

Another change is that marriages are far more likely to end in divorce or separation than used to be the case. **d** It is estimated that more than four in ten (42%) of marriages will now end in divorce, half of them in the first ten years of marriage. Successive changes in the divorce laws making divorce easier and available to all have led to increases in the divorce rate. Another reflection of changes in society is the fact that 65% of divorces are granted to women. Divorce shows that people are less likely to remain in a marriage that is no longer happy, which could mean that people now have high expectations of marriage and are prepared to end it if it doesn't live up to what they think it should be. Divorce does not mean that people no longer value marriage – a third of all marriages taking place involve a second marriage for at least one of the partners, as mentioned in the Item. **e** This also helps to explain the rise in the average age of marriage. **f** However, it does mean that, unlike for most people in the past, marriage is not necessarily seen as being for ever.

e **d** The second change to be discussed is spelled out, followed by some good analysis. **e and f** Material from the Item is identified and used to make the link between divorce, remarriage and the average age of marriage. Note that reference to the same material in the Item (a rise in the average age of marriage) has been used in both parts of the question. **10/10 marks awarded.**

---

3 The idea that a particular family form is the best 'fit' for a particular type of society is a functionalist view. **a** Functionalists believe that each institution (or 'organ') of society has a particular role to play in maintaining a stable society. Sometimes changes in society will lead to changes in either the roles or structures of the different parts of society. **b**

---

e **a** A correct identification of the view expressed in the question. **b** Followed by a brief general explanation of functionalism.

Functionalists such as Parsons believe that certain family types are best suited to particular economic structures. In non-industrial societies, when work is highly labour-intensive and most goods are made by hand, they believe that close-knit extended families, working together, are the best type of family structure to meet the needs of that type of society. With industrialisation and urbanisation, though, there is a need for a smaller, more geographically mobile type of family unit that moves away from rural areas to work in the developing mechanised industries. Therefore it is suggested that a nuclear family is the most suitable for industrialised societies. **c**

---

e **c** Further explanation of the functionalist view, well focused on the question. It is important not to spend too long on lengthy explanations.

The argument goes further than this though. Functionalists believe that not only family structure but family roles should adapt. Parsons believed that as the state took over many of the former functions of the family, the two most important ones remained, and these were the socialisation of children and what he called the 'stabilisation of the adult personalities'. It is these two functions that are referred to in the Item. **d** The idea of 'home-centred' also touches on another functionalist idea, that is that male and female roles in the family are complementary, with men as the breadwinners and decision-makers and women as the nurturing, caring partner whose focus is the home and the children. **e**

---

e **d and e** Appropriate reference is made to material in the Item, again linking it to the functionalist view, with some further elaboration.

The idea that family breakdown leads to the kinds of social ills referred to in the Item (i.e. delinquency and anti-social behaviour) is associated with New Right thinkers such as Charles Murray, whose ideas have been adopted by many politicians both here and in the United States. **f** The claims are that women spending much of their time in paid employment and rising rates of divorce and separation mean not only stress for adults but poor parenting. Parents have insufficient time to discipline their children properly and/or too many children are brought up by a lone (often unmarried) mother without a father figure in the home. This, it is argued, leads boys in particular to develop anti-social and even criminal behaviour. Some New Right thinkers go further and claim that family breakdown and the decline of the nuclear family with two (married) parents is also the cause of other social problems such as teenage pregnancies, poor attitudes to education and a 'culture of dependency', by which they mean an acceptance of life on benefits without even trying to find employment. **g**

e **f** Good use is made of other material in the Item. **g** There is further explanation and analysis.

How far do these arguments stand up? If we look at the idea that the 'traditional nuclear family' best meets the needs of its members, then this is not always the case. For functionalists, 'traditional nuclear family' means 'traditional gender roles', and there is plenty of research to show that these are not good for everybody. Sociologists such as Oakley and others have shown that many women are unhappy and frustrated with a purely domestic role. Equally, many men have complained that they would like to play a greater part in looking after their children and spending more leisure time with their family. There is no evidence that those who cohabit are any less happy than married couples, and that those who choose to remain single are generally as happy as those who live as a couple. Equally, the growing number of same-sex couples shows that other family forms can be just as fulfilling. Other ways in which the 'traditional nuclear family' may not always be the ideal for its members is shown by the fact that there are very high rates of domestic violence in society, and many children who have suffered physical and/or sexual abuse have experienced it from family members. **h**

e **h** The answer now moves to an evaluation of the view expressed in the question by citing some evidence against the view.

Families are just one of the agencies that socialise young children – schools, peer groups and the media have a role to play. **i** The fact that many children from lone-parent families do not do as well as other children usually owes more to the fact that such families are often in poverty than to inadequate parenting. **j**

e **i** Another very brief mention of something provided in the Item (socialisation) though not developed. **j** The point about children in lone-parent families, while accurate and potentially relevant, is not clearly linked to the question.

Marxists would claim that the traditional nuclear family is held as the ideal because it best serves the needs of capitalism, by raising the next generation of workers and using the unpaid labour of women to help (male) workers cope with the alienating experiences of work. Feminists would claim that the traditional nuclear family oppresses women and certainly does not work to their benefit. **k**

e **k** Bringing in the ideas of Marxists and feminists provides a good opportunity for evaluation of the functionalist view, but these are just stated and not developed.

There are currently many different types of family in Britain, and little real evidence to show that any one type best serves the interests of its members and of society as a whole. **l**

e **l** A rather weak conclusion that tries to answer the question but adds little. **16/20 marks awarded.**

Overall mark: 36/40

Student B

1   One way in which household structures has changed is that they contain fewer children. **a** Over the past hundred years the average number of children per family has fallen. Although there are still variations by social class and ethnicity, the average number of children per family is now one or two. **b and c** Even though high rates of infant mortality in the past meant that many babies and young children died, average families were larger than today. **d**

e **a** An appropriate change identified, though the subsequent discussion should be longer and more detailed. **b** Although class and ethnic variations are mentioned, there is no explanation of what these variations are. **c** Some indication should have been given of what the average number of children was 100 years ago. **d** Although appropriate reference is made to high rates of infant mortality, there should be a reference to higher birth rates to explain why despite infant deaths, families were usually larger than they are today.

Another change in household structures is that most households now consist of a single nuclear family. **e** In the past, the poor would have often lived with other families, related or not, while the wealthy would have had live-in servants. **f** If you look at the Census returns for individual districts in the 1851 Census, and if the district is a working-class one, you will see lots of cases with more than one family at the same address, and also many poor families had young single men living with them as lodgers. **g** High death rates, especially among the poor, also meant that many households contained widowed relatives, male or female, and their children. If both parents had died, then some families would be looking after the orphaned children of relatives, to stop them having to go to the orphanages. **h**

ⓔ **e** A second appropriate change is identified. **f** A difference in household composition between poor and wealthy families is pointed out. **g** Reference to the 1851 Census falls outside the time frame, although the point being made would still have been valid 100 years ago. **h** The paragraph concludes with some examples of reasons for mixed households.

Overall, a competent though undeveloped answer. **5/10 marks awarded.**

> **2** As the Item says, marriage as an institution remains strong, though there have been many changes. **a** The growth of secularisation in society **b** means that most marriages now don't take place in church – in fact, many now take place in hotels and stately homes.

ⓔ **a** There is no point in simply copying out a sentence from the Item – the examiner will be looking to see whether and how you have used (applied) the material. There is a reference to civil ceremonies, but this is not specifically linked to the Item (always show the examiner that you are using the material). **b** The point about increasing secularisation could have been developed and made into one of the changes.

> As the Item says, many marriages are not first marriages but are a remarriage for at least one of the partners. **c** This is because of the number of people who get married, get divorced and then remarry, something known as serial monogamy. **d** This is a change in society, because most people used to get married only once. **e** Even when it became easier to divorce, many people stayed in unhappy marriages because divorce was still thought of as rather shocking, and it used to be quite difficult for a divorced woman, especially if she had children, to manage to live without the financial support of a man. The fact that most women are now used to going out to work and earning, even when married and with children, and the fact that there are benefits for lone parents, as well as ways to try to get fathers to contribute to the upbringing of their children, means that both divorce and remarriage are now more common. **f**

ⓔ **c** Again, material is simply copied from the Item. **d and e** The next point is relevant, shows basic analysis and introduces a relevant concept, which is then linked to a change in patterns of marriage. **f** The last section develops this and shows analysis.

> Another change is there has been a rise in the average age at marriage. **g** This is because more females are going into higher education and wanting their own career before settling down to marriage and a family. Men too are delaying getting married, mainly for financial reasons. Many young men (and women) go back home to live with their parents as they can't afford to live independently, and this again will delay their marriage. **h**

e **g** No reference is made to the Item, though this is where the material comes from. **h** The reasons given for both women and men are accurate but basic and not developed. **4/10 marks awarded.**

---

3 Functionalists believe that the nuclear family is best for industrial societies, where there is a need for a mobile workforce and where the state has taken over some older functions of the family such as looking after older relatives and caring for the sick. **a**

---

e **a** Correct identification of the view expressed in the question.

For any society to survive, people must be socialised into the norms and values of that society, such as learning the language and what is considered right and wrong. Functionalists such as Parsons thought that the socialisation of children and the stabilisation of adult personalities were the two essential functions that were carried out by nuclear families. His ideas were based on 1950s' America. **b**

---

e **b** This is good, but should have been linked to the Item, to show that relevant material has been applied and developed. It is not made clear how the fact that Parsons' ideas were based on 1950s' America is relevant.

Some politicians have been influenced by New Right thinkers such as Charles Murray, who looked at Britain and claimed that lots of social problems such as delinquency and other forms of anti-social behaviour are caused by the breakdown of the traditional nuclear family, as it says in the Item. **c** David Cameron, the Prime Minister, set up the 'Troubled Families' initiative after the urban riots of 2011 because he believed that this kind of family caused a disproportionate amount of problems in society and also cost the tax payer a great deal of money. Some of these families are actually nuclear in structure. **d**

---

e **c** Use of the material in the Item and accurately linked to the New Right. **d** Some linked analysis and evaluation by reference to a particular social policy.

Firstly, is it true that this type of problem comes from or is caused by family breakdown? There are two arguments here. One is that not all families who have suffered breakdown end up causing problems – some family members are probably happier and more stable as it is sometimes better to break up than to live in a family where there are lots of rows and unhappiness. e Secondly, the crime and anti-social behaviour statistics that show the perpetrators as coming from largely working-class families in deprived areas are high because levels of policing are higher in these areas and the police are known to have stereotypes of young working-class males, especially blacks, and may ignore or be unaware of anti-social behaviour committed by wealthier middle-class youths from 'good' families, such as some of the antics of Oxbridge undergraduates. f

e e Some relevant evaluation. f It is not made clear how the following points are relevant to the discussion of family types, though there is possibly implicit reference to 'troubled families'.

Not all nuclear families are good for their members. There is a lot of domestic violence and child abuse that goes on in families 'behind closed doors'. Feminists would say that traditional families exploit women. g We also can't say that the traditional nuclear family is best for society, as there are now so many other types of family and household in Britain, and we can't say that the problems that we have in society are all because we don't have more nuclear families. Think of the ways that the austerity programme is harming people – and the cause of that was capitalism and greedy and immoral bankers! h

e g Some evaluation of nuclear families and their members, though the point about feminists could have been developed. h Further evaluation relating to nuclear families and society.

Overall, when they work well, traditional nuclear families are good for the people in them and therefore good for society, but this is not always the case, and it is not to say that other types of family structure can't and don't work just as well. i

e i A reasonably good conclusion that attempts to answer the question and follows from the arguments and evidence presented. 16/20 marks awarded.

Overall mark: 25/40

Practice questions

The following two questions, one for AS and one for A-level, are for you to try, though some guidance is given for the higher-mark questions. A good way of using these is to make notes and do appropriate revision, then put away all your notes and books and write the answer in the appropriate time, which is roughly an hour. If you can get a friend to do the same thing and then 'mark' and discuss and compare your answers, you will find this particularly helpful.

Question 1 (AS)

1   Define the term 'reconstituted family'.   (2 marks)

2   Using one example, briefly explain how the increase in family breakdown can affect household structure.   (2 marks)

3   Outline three reasons for the fall in the birth rate over the past century.   (2 marks)

4   Outline and explain two ways in which the roles of women have changed over the past 70 years.   (10 marks)

   ⓔ This time period is roughly from the end of the Second World War – don't go further back than that.

5   Read Item A below and answer the question that follows.

Item A
Many sociologists claim that changes such as the increase in the length of time in compulsory education and a better understanding of child development have resulted in a great improvement in the quality of life for children. Others, however, point to negative factors such as the growing commercialisation of childhood.

   Applying material from Item A and your knowledge, evaluate the view that the experience of childhood has greatly improved over the past century.   (20 marks)

   ⓔ Make sure that you make use of all the relevant material in the Item – and stick to the time period indicated.

Question 2 (A-level)

1   Outline and explain two reasons for the fall in the fertility rate over the past century.   (10 marks)

   ⓔ Make quite sure that it is the fertility rate that you discuss.

2   Read Item B below and answer the question that follows.

Item B
Functionalist sociologists believe that extended family structures are best suited to pre-industrial societies when work was based on the household and people needed the support of kin in most areas of life. They anticipated that with industrialisation, extended families would be replaced by nuclear families. Others, however, believe that extended family structures have changed rather than disappeared.

Applying material from Item B, analyse two changes in extended family structures over the past century.

(10 marks)

ⓔ Remember that this is about the structure of 'extended' families.

3 Read Item C below and answer the question that follows.

Item C

Marxists believe that an important role of the family in capitalist society is to socialise members into accepting the ideas of the ruling class and adopting values such as obedience to authority.

The role of women is also seen as important, as they raise the next generation of workers, but their domestic labour is unpaid.

Applying material from Item C and your own knowledge, evaluate the Marxist view of the role of the family in capitalist society.

(20 marks)

ⓔ Make sure that you use (apply) all the material provided for you in the Item.

Knowledge check answers

1 Almost everywhere else, but primarily at school, in the media and among peer groups.

2 Childless couples; lone-parent families; same-sex couples.

3 The evidence doesn't really support this at all. Children tend to be socialised into gender roles rather than them occurring 'naturally', and many adult men and women do not conform to them. Also gender roles differ between societies, emphasising the fact that they are culturally defined.

4 The practice by which one can have only one legal spouse at a time.

5 Rather than families producing goods and services (units of production) they now buy manufactured goods and other services for use by families – they have become consumers.

6 Lone parents do not conform to the socially desirable two-parent nuclear family, and workless households rely on the state for their income rather than generating at least some of it through work (as some politicians have remarked, 'shirkers not workers'). Note that the underlying assumption here is that both these family forms are a choice rather than a result of circumstances.

7 Industrialisation refers to the process by which a society moves from being primarily agricultural where most goods and services are provided by the extended family household to one in which most goods are manufactured in specialised locations and many services are bought in or provided by the state. Urbanisation refers to the process in which there is a movement of the population from rural areas to living in towns and cities.

8 A forced marriage is one in which at least one of the parties has not given their free consent. An arranged marriage is one in which someone else – a family member or a specialist agent – has played a part in bringing the couple together.

9 The crude birth rate is the number of live births per thousand of the population in a given year. The total fertility rate is the average total number of children women in a population will have over their child-bearing period – usually calculated as between the ages of 15 and 45.

10 Reasons include: many people in this age group are recently divorced; lone parents whose children have moved away from home; in the upper age limit, people who have been widowed.

11 Essential labour that is carried out within the home, e.g. housework, cooking, caring for children.

12 Conflict that occurs when the demands of work (e.g. working overtime, or not being absent) conflict with family demands (e.g. looking after a sick child, wanting to go to see a child's school play, needing to take an elderly parent to a medical appointment).

13 If women as well as their partners are breadwinners (and they may be the only or higher-earning breadwinner) they may feel greater entitlement to share in household decision-making, and may feel it reasonable to insist that their partner take a greater share of domestic labour.

14 Reasons include fear of further violence if the crime is reported; feelings of shame or guilt; concern that the complaint may not be taken seriously by police.

15 Those from confidential self-completion surveys – using a computer will allow people to express things that they might be reluctant to speak about if answering face to face.

16 Roles performed by the adults in a marriage or relationship, particularly with reference to domestic labour, childcare, decision-making and leisure pursuits.

17 A crime that is often not reported by victims (or if reported not acted upon) and not brought to the attention of police, the media and the general public.

18 There is a large Roman Catholic population in Northern Ireland, and because of the attitude of the Catholic Church towards contraception, family sizes tend to be larger.

19 A population in which the proportion of people in the older age groups is usually as high or higher than that in the youngest groups.

20 Older people are less likely to have grown up with many immigrants in their local population. Middle-class people may feel less threatened by immigrants than working-class people who fear they will lose jobs to immigrants who may be prepared to work for lower wages.

21 The difference between the number of people leaving a country to live elsewhere (emigration) and the number coming into a country (immigration).

22 The increasing number of ways in which societies are linked together – economically, politically and socially.

23 Primary data is information that the researcher has gathered for themselves; secondary data are information that already exists, e.g. official statistics, written reports.

24 A structured interview has set questions that are asked in the same order to everyone; an unstructured interview occurs when the researcher has a general list of questions, often not written down, and is able to 'depart from the script' if the respondent raises other issues.

25 A study in which the original sample of people are re-interviewed or given another questionnaire at regular intervals throughout a given period of time.

Index